BOHEMIAN STYLE at HOME

On the cover:

Front: Photo by Paulina Arcklin www.paulinaarcklin.net /
   Courtesy Zoco Home www.zocohome.com.

Back: Wicker ball lamp by Nedgis, courtesy of HK Living;
   Peacock Chair, courtesy of Out There Interiors

First published in the United Kingdom in 2019 by
Thames & Hudson Ltd, 181A High Holborn, London WC1V 7QX

This book was designed and produced by
The Bright Press, an imprint of the Quarto Group
The Old Brewery
6 Blundell Street
London N7 9BH

British Library Cataloguing-in-Publication Data
A catalogue record for this book is available from the British Library

ISBN 978-0-500-29498-7

Printed and bound in China

To find out about all our publications, please visit **www.thamesandhudson.com**.
There you can subscribe to our e-newsletter, browse or download our current
catalogue, and buy any titles that are in print.

A ROOM BY ROOM GUIDE

BOHEMIAN
STYLE
at HOME

Kate Young

Thames & Hudson

Contents

Preface

Forget trend forecasts, colour of the year or the latest fad – bohemian style is all about telling your story and being as creative as you like. Every bohemian home is as unique as the person who creates it and the only things they all have in common are a lack of formality, an incredible sense of wellbeing and a big dose of unrestrained recklessness.

Having travelled extensively in my twenties, I had fully embraced the carefree, non-materialistic bohemian lifestyle. Upon returning home, my first flat was a shrine to all those colourful textiles and hand-crafted goods and keepsakes I had brought back with me.

In early 2000, long before the explosion of the Scandi boho frenzy, I became increasingly interested in interior design. I was keen to explore new trends and, in particular, the then relatively new and undiscovered Scandinavian style, but somehow it always felt too clinical and sterile for me. I wanted to introduce some of the textures I had discovered in Morocco and India without necessarily having the riot of colours and patterns that had dominated my first home.

In this book, I will show you the different takes on bohemian design – whether you are a minimalist Scandinavian, glam, rustic, mid-century maximalist or colour lover – and how you can adapt the style to suit your tastes, needs and budget. The room-by-room guide will give you the key to mastering bohemian style – something that is often perceived as hard to get right simply because it lacks hard-and-fast design 'rules'.

▶ *This sun-filled Floridian bedroom mixes a vivid colour palette and a variety of natural materials – including a Buddha bamboo lamp – against the striking backdrop of a tropical rainforest mural.*

1. INTRODUCING
BOHEMIAN STYLE

What is bohemian style?

The term 'bohemian style' is bandied about a lot and often applies to a decorating approach characterized by free-flowing fabrics, bright colours and a multitude of clashing patterns. Heavily inspired by the 1960s and 1970s free-spirited way of life, it is one of the most versatile styles of decoration. Sometimes rule-breaking and always personal, it could best be described as a way to live in complete harmony with your surroundings. Forget about famous designers and carefully planned decorating schemes, boho is the antipode of trends.

While the 'anything goes' approach is meant to be liberating, the prospect of having no rules to abide by can be daunting when trying to recreate bohemian style for yourself. There are however a few key elements that define a true bohemian home:

Vintage

Vintage furniture and accessories are an essential component of bohemian design and will give your home that authentic look. Flea markets, charity shops and salvage yards are great places to start hunting for unique pieces.

Texture

We often think of bohemian design as a feast of colour, but texture features just as heavily in the scheme. In fact, it's possible to achieve a bohemian look with very little colour as long as you pile on the textures.

Plants

In a bid to blur the boundaries between the inside and outside world and be completely at one with nature, the bohemian home is always crammed with plants.

Soulfulness and creativity

Boho style is about following your heart and guts. Infuse your personal taste into your decor and you will have a bohemian home as individual as you are.

▲ *Plants are an inexpensive way to add colour to a room. Here they add a welcoming touch to this entryway.*

▶ *To add interest to a small space, choose unusual ways to hang plants from the ceiling.*

The history of bohemian design

Bohemian style is often associated with the hippie trend of the 1960s and 1970s, but it goes much further than that. It is a culture and a state of mind, a melting pot of different influences that go as far back as the 19th century. For us to understand better what boho is, it is necessary to look at the roots of these influences. Only then can we understand the diversity and eclecticism that embodies this style.

The Bohemians

The word 'bohemian' originates from the Czech province of Bohemia. For centuries, Bohemia was the centre of much political, cultural and religious discord. To escape this turmoil, outspoken artists and musicians began making their way to France, where a Bohemian counterculture was born. At its core was a sense of freedom from the middle class and rebellion against its materialistic values. French bourgeois youths and impoverished artists joined the movement and became the first generation of Bohemians. Brought together by the same yearning to pursue an artistic way of life, they lived a penniless, carefree existence.

The Hippies

In the 1950s, the Beat movement and hippie subcultures were searching for the same freedom and non-conformism as the Bohemians. In the

1970s, in a bid to break out of a rigid, conventional lifestyle, hippies hitchhiked their way from London to Kathmandu and beyond in search of spiritual enlightenment. Their persistent questioning of authority and accepted rules constitute the foundations of bohemian design.

The core principles

With such a colourful and diverse background, it should come as no surprise that bohemian design is as varied as it is. Unlike other forms of design, there are no rules to abide by. It is therefore impossible to pinpoint a specific designer or colour scheme to define boho. Instead, its foundation is based on a strong ideology which united people from across the globe – people who were all in search of the same free-spirited, laid-back and individual way of life.

▲ The bold 1970s wall hanging above the bed acts as a headboard and creates a colourful and striking focal point.

◄ The covered terrace with a large hanging chair provides somewhere to sit all year round. The abundance of natural materials connects the room with the garden.

Early bohemian decor

Armed with that 'anything goes, no rules' attitude, early bohemian decor was a bold and colourful affair, an invasion of greenery along with some memorable pieces of furniture like the iconic Hans Wegner PP130 circle chair. The carpet pile was high, and the sofas were low. Times change, but bohemian design remains as cool and unique as ever.

The evolution of bohemian design

Interest in bohemian design has ebbed and flowed through the years, and its renewed level of popularity today may be due to the merging of various decorating styles. Some argue that the style is mutating into a diluted version of itself, but the essence of bohemian design remains – it is simply adapting to suit modern tastes and lifestyles.

▲ *This Scandinavian take on boho contrasts the austerity of the grey floor and the white fridge with an exuberantly vibrant wallpaper.*

▶ *A grand ornate mirror and large oil painting transform this living room into boho chic heaven.*

Scandinavian boho

This may seem to many an impossible combination, but Scandinavian boho has made bohemian design much more accessible by reining in the exuberant colour schemes and curbing maximalism. By the same token, the once cold, formal Scandinavian style has warmed up somewhat and now produces interiors that are focusing slightly more on form than function.

The look Keep the backdrop simple with white walls, but introduce plenty of textures like classic Berber rugs, throws and cushions. Add the obligatory greenery and warm up the whole scheme with rustic wood and stylish vintage furniture.

Haute bohemian

A relatively new permutation of bohemian style, haute bohemian can best be described as boho getting itself an upgrade to first class. First seen in Miguel Flores Vianna's book *Haute Bohemians*, the style's core principle remains, but the whole look is far more restrained, structured and carefully curated.

The look Here, the location is everything, and is usually a grand affair – think country house, chateau, palazzo.

Industrial boho

Mixing cold exposed steel with the warmth of wood and vibrant textures and colours, bohemian design moves into lofts and industrial buildings. The stark contrast of materials achieves a perfect aesthetic balance.

The look Distressed brick walls are adorned with eclectic art, concrete floors are softened with thick layers of rugs and the exposed steel is enhanced by lush greenery.

Boho luxe

A more modernized take on boho, this look is sleeker and exudes a more lavish, elegant, 'put together' feel.

The look Layer metallic mirrors and lamps with wood or rattan. Pair up a marble table next to a luxurious velvet sofa.

Monochrome boho

This may be one shift too far for many boho aficionados, but let's remember bohemian design follows no rules. The maximalist side of boho remains in monochrome boho, but all the colours have disappeared to make space for a bigger emphasis on texture.

The look Except for botanical touches, all colour is banished. The once brightly coloured Aztec prints are now black and white.

▲ *The layering of textures replaces the traditional vibrant colours in this monochrome boho space.*

◄ *A simple mattress on the floor and oversized pillows soften the distressed brick wall in this industrial boho living room.*

2. ACHIEVING THE LOOK

Welcome to the bohemian home

Richly textured, artistic, eclectic and unique, the bohemian home will make you feel welcome the moment you step through the door. Its comfortable, lived-in feel draws you in and soothes your senses. Forget immaculate and spurious, the boho home exudes harmony and a certain nonchalance. This home isn't about flawless design and careful styling; it's about the people who live there and their sense of adventure, their history and their journey so far. Once inside, you will feel compelled to know more.

First impressions

The hallway of a bohemian home sets the tone for the rest of the house. It entices you with its thick rugs, impossibly cool artwork and the copious number of vintage mirrors. Plants are hanging from the ceiling and the Chinese lantern lighting is soft. A mid-century side table displays books and randomly collected items. You can smell the incense burning and you know you are never going to want to leave this place. Welcome to the bohemian home.

Living

The living room is the hub of the house and it is full of vibrant colours punctuated by a plethora of textiles such as tasselled throws, Moroccan cushions and whimsical lace curtains. The seating arrangement is casual and comfortable. Low, sectional sofas are often a favoured option. The room is adorned with art, handmade macramé wall hangings and personal keepsakes and photos. The furniture is a mix of vintage and repurposed pieces. Plants are abundant and bring the room to life. Candlelight is often preferred to harsh overhead lighting.

◄ *Small, round dining room tables are perfect when space is tight as bohemian homes are always sociable.*

► *Bring the outdoors in with a hammock and plenty of plants.*

▸ *Create your own little bohemian space with a shaggy throw, some colourful Aztec pillows and an abundance of plants.*

▸▸ *Use furniture to create smaller zones in an open-plan space.*

Eating

Forget the practicalities of fitted units, the bohemian kitchen is a mix of mismatched cupboards and crockery all displayed on open shelving as yet another collection of family heirlooms and kitchen curios. A rustic table strewed with candles and surrounded by mismatched chairs completes the look.

Sleeping

The boho bedroom is more than just a place to lay your head at night. Rich in textures like crumpled linen, sumptuous velvets and worldly textiles, the bed is the focal point. Clothes are displayed in open wardrobes and jewellery is hanging on the walls. Rugs are layered, and the bed is low.

Cleaning

There is nothing sleek or clinical about the bohemian bathroom, as this room is treated much like the rest of the house when it comes to furnishings. You will even see art on the walls. Free-standing baths are usually the preferred option and vintage curtains and rugs are often plentiful. The sink will be found in a repurposed console table and a large ornate antique mirror will hang above it.

Colour palette

It is almost impossible to think of bohemian design without its vast array of bold, bright, clashing colours and abundantly rich patterns. The lack of rules means there is no prescribed colour palette to stick to and really nothing is off limits.

The trademark colours traditionally include the brightest oranges, purples, pinks, reds and greens, and whilst the bohemian colour palette today still showcases all of these bright and sometimes over-the-top colours, there is an increasing amount of earthy neutral tones thrown into the mix, which counterbalances the intensity of the scheme.

The backdrop

In contrast to the myriad colours found in the textiles and accessories, the backdrop of a boho home can be a neutral, sometimes pared-back affair. Raw plaster, distressed bricks or just plain

◄ *The dark walls provide a striking background, creating a very earthy feel in this sitting room.*

▲ *This double-height space is made more intimate by the use of long, fluid pieces such as the wall hanging, knotted lampshade and plant holders.*

most varied in the design world. From mid-century muted greens and soft blues to 1970s vibrant orange and warm browns, every colour has a place in a boho home.

Using colour

Whilst most bohemian interiors appear to display a riot of colours, there is a method to the madness of the scheme: by picking a maximum of two or three colours in a room and adding different hues of those colours, you will retain a sense of flow and unity throughout. It is important for any decorating scheme to leave somewhere for the eyes to rest, so why not choose to paint the floor or the ceiling instead of the walls? Other ways to inject colour into a room include painting furniture and using colourful rugs, cushions, throws and even flowers to spruce things up.

Mixing colours and patterns

With no colour or pattern out of bounds, retaining that cohesive look can be a challenge. There are a couple of ways to do this: the first is to choose one inspirational piece, such as a painting, and pull all the colours from that piece. This approach will enable you to mix and layer patterns with reckless abandon, from ikat cushions to Suzani throws and Kantha curtains, without abandoning a sense of continuity. The second approach is to choose patterns that relate to each other. For example, you could group ethnic or floral patterns together. This scheme will allow you to be bolder with your colour choices whilst still retaining overall cohesion.

▲ *A bright purple carpet injects vibrancy into this living room. The dark walls make the art stand out and cushions complete this maximalist boho space.*

▶ *A wall mural adds instant interest and depth to this subdued colour palette.*

white walls gives the look a nod to its more modest roots and will bring balance to an otherwise pattern-filled scheme.

The signature colours

Bohemian interiors are inspired by many different cultures and eras, making the signature colours the

Bohemian furniture

A bohemian's home is a maximalist's dream and will be filled with many pieces of furniture – mostly second-hand vintage pieces or items brought back from various parts of the world. Whilst the size and shape of the furniture is not important, it is vital that every single piece is steeped in history. Unlike most other types of decor, there is no specific designer to keep in mind, and you can mix and match eras and styles. A coffee table from Morocco will sit quite happily side by side a 1965 Florence Knoll sideboard or a pair of Pieff Alpha leather chairs. So, if anything goes, how do you begin to furnish your bohemian home? Well, even though there are no defining designers, there are a few pieces that over the years have become intrinsically linked to bohemian design and will help you achieve a look that is eclectic, bold and as individual as you are.

Exotic pieces

As we have seen, the history of bohemian design is a varied and colourful one. In the 1970s, India and Morocco were regarded as enviable, exotic destinations for bohemian culture, but though it has always drawn from culturally rich countries, boho style has never been confined geographically. It's also not just the textiles from places like Asia, North Africa and the Middle East that are gracing boho interiors, but beautiful and intricately carved pieces of furniture too.

5 pieces to buy

▷ A Chakki table
▷ Indian mirrors
▷ Moroccan tea tray tables
▷ A Damchiya cabinet
▷ Zouak hand-painted tables

◄ *Vintage furniture can be given a new lease of life with a coat of paint.*

► *An old worn-out chair provides just the right amount of contrast in this grand living room.*

▲ The oversized wicker shade is hung low to create a soft ambience.

▶ Don't be afraid to mix and match different styles of furniture. Here a simple rattan chair sits alongside a gold table to create an eclectic corner in a sitting room.

Wicker

Made popular in the early 20th century by Heywood-Wakefield, wicker is best described as a style of weaving. It is made from cheap plants and grasses such as rattan, cane, bamboo or even straw. It features heavily in the bohemian home, where wicker furniture, baskets and even lighting can be found in abundance.

One of the most popular pieces of bohemian wicker furniture is the peacock chair (see pages 136-7). In fact, it is one of the bohemian style trademarks. Both vintage and new wicker pieces are easy to source from second-hand or high street stores and are relatively cheap.

6 pieces to buy

▷ A peacock chair
▷ A wicker plant stand
▷ Wicker cane tub chairs
▷ A rattan dividing screen
▷ A hanging chair
▷ A bamboo wardrobe

Mid-century furniture

On first impression, it is hard to see how the somewhat austere design of mid-century furniture would fit into the anti-minimalist, free-spirited bohemian home. But boho design is all about contrast and history, and mid-century furniture offers both.

5 pieces to buy

▷ A G-plan dining table

▷ Pieff Delta chrome chairs

▷ An Ercol Elm stick back Goldsmith chair

▷ A teak sideboard (perfect for displaying a multitude of plants, books and showcasing your own personal collections)

▷ A chrome and leather sling chair

▼ *The iconic 1960s Inca chair by Swedish designer Arne Norell.*

▶ *The Camaleonda sofa designed by Mario Bellini is a 1970s classic.*

A nod to the 1970s

The simultaneously rebellious, carefree
and laid-back feel of the 1970s is one that is
captured time and time again in bohemian design.
The modular low seating arrangements popular
then remain a firm favourite in the sociable
bohemian home.

5 pieces to buy

▷ A Ligne Roset Togo sofa

▷ A Barcelona chair

▷ The De Sede DS70 leather sofa

▷ The Geoffrey Harcourt F504 lounge chair

▷ A vinyl record stand

The art of thrifting

Thrifting is not so much about finding cheap items to furnish your home (although that's always a bonus), but more about the thrill of finding something with a little bit of history attached to it, salvaging it and giving it a new lease of life. It's about hunting down a piece and the joy of finally finding it. It's about making your home a unique and eclectic place that will reflect your own individual style. Here are a few tips on how to thrift effectively:

▷ If you are looking for large items of furniture, measure the space you have at home first. This will save you buying items on impulse and then finding you have no place for them to go. For the same reason, always carry a tape measure. Consider repainting and/or reupholstering pieces that are not exactly to your taste. A fresh pair of eyes and a lick of paint might be all it takes to bring tired-looking items back to life.

▷ If you are shopping online, be sure to ask a lot of questions about the condition of the item you wish to purchase, including its history. And remember that photographs aren't always a true representation.

▷ Go with your gut: if you love it then you can make it work.

▷ Think laterally. A 1970s tablecloth could easily become a curtain; a vintage bread basket might make an interesting wall decoration. When it comes to thrifting, it's all about being resourceful.

▷ Be prepared to rummage, and get your hands dirty if need be. It's a well-known fact that the best treasures are usually buried under mountains of other stuff.

▷ Be patient. Don't get disheartened if you can't find anything worth buying at first. The thrill of the discovery comes with time.

▷ Google is your friend. If you get the feeling you're about to be ripped off, check online by comparing the prices of similar pieces.

▷ Don't be afraid to negotiate; it's part of the experience. Remember to bring cash with you too, as it always helps when trying to get a good deal.

▷ Finally, enjoy the process; it is the most satisfying way to shop bar none.

▲ *A collection of vases have been arranged on this piano to create a colourful display.*

The art of display

Bohemian design is all about making your home a reflection of who you are, and nothing does that better than displaying anything and everything that you treasure. Psychologists call it 'behavioural residue', the idea that your home lets the world know who you are. Keepsakes, holiday snaps, personal collections, maps to chronicle your travels, artwork or just beautiful everyday objects – anything can be turned into an art installation. Think of every object as an opportunity to showcase your personality.

It's important to keep in mind, however, that within all this chaos, there must be some semblance of order, and you don't want your house to look like a garage sale. The key to avoiding this is what's called curating, which involves much more than simply choosing pretty things to be displayed.

Curating

Curating, quite simply, is the process of selecting, organising and displaying the items you have collected. There is no set formula to follow since it mostly relies on instinct rather than rules, but here are a few tips and tricks that will ensure your collections make a big impact:

Where to display your collections There is a vast choice of display cabinets that will work in your bohemian home. Whether you choose vintage or new, ones with or without doors, keep the design simple to really highlight its contents. Don't limit yourself to displaying curios inside cupboards. Look around you and turn window sills, coffee tables, open shelving, even staircases into beautiful vignettes.

▲ *Vintage lampshades create a quirky display.*

What to display Anything and everything that you treasure is fair game in a boho abode. Even the most mundane, everyday items can be turned into an exciting and personal art display. From wooden spoons to fabrics, coloured glass to hats, the only narrative is that the objects mean something to you.

Here are a few examples:

▷ Coloured glass
▷ Enamelware
▷ Books
▷ Chopping boards
▷ Vintage clothing
▷ Plates
▷ Maps
▷ Vinyls
▷ Baskets
▷ Cameras

▲ When creating a vignette, combine a variety of colours, patterns, textures and materials to create interest.

can be a big part of our identity and our clothes don't need to be hidden just because we're not wearing them. A silk kimono can be hung simply on the wall next to a painting; take jewellery out of its box and display it proudly on a cork board or stand; cowboy boots can be left out to be admired rather than buried in a closet. Nothing is off limits in a bohemian home.

Displaying art

Whether you create a piece of art or spend thousands in a gallery, whether you're dealing with children's drawings or a rare oil painting, art is yet another layer to your bohemian home and should be present in every room, even the kitchen and bathroom.

What to display Don't just hang pictures on your walls; remember, variety is the spice of bohemian design. Hang rugs and tapestries, frame beautiful vintage fabrics, book pages and objects like old cameras, shoe lasts and vintage tools. These objects will add textural interest to your walls. Separate art and frames for a more interesting display.

How to display your collections The first step is to find a unifying trait, an element that connects all the objects. That could be a colour, a material, a texture or even an experience (you could group together everything you found beachcombing, for instance). This will help to balance the appearance of your collection and avoid garage-sale territory.

Showcasing clothes

Displaying your clothes is a very effective way of turning an everyday item – a coat, dress, bag or even a pair of shoes – into a work of art. Fashion

Where to shop Flea markets, junk shops and local art galleries as well as places like Etsy are all great places to find original art.

How to display Mix and match how you display your art. Hang in vintage frames, lean casually against a wall or just use masking tape to showcase a favourite photograph. Finally, think about layering pieces of art, maybe casually leaning one against another. This will add depth to your display and help to create an intriguing and interesting bohemian home.

Plants

Plants may have seen a huge revival in the design world in the past few years, but they have always been a boho staple! After all, one of the key elements in bohemian design is its connection with nature. Adding greenery will instantly liven up a space and help to blur the boundaries between indoors and outdoors as well as suggesting a sense of wellbeing. But that's not the only reason to consider turning your home into a mini jungle. Plants will also add colour, texture and even pattern, thus creating more layers and interest in your boho abode.

Welcome to the jungle

The maximalist side of bohemian design really comes into its own with plants. Create your own little indoor garden by grouping plants together in mix-and-match containers. Lavish every available nook and cranny with a plethora of plants; hang them in baskets, display them on windowsills and coffee tables – you could even dedicate a whole bookshelf to plants.

Go big

The biggest plants make the most impact and will provide a focal point to your room. Some of the larger specimens include:

▷ The umbrella tree (*Schefflera arboricola*), which needs bright but indirect sunlight.

▷ The Norfolk Island pine (*Araucaria heterophylla*), a tropical plant that likes humid conditions. It can reach 2–3 metres in height.

▷ The Kentia palm (*Howea forsteriana*). Elegant and easy to care for, it will tolerate most conditions.

▷ The fiddle-fig leaf (*Ficus lyrata*) is slow-growing

and likes moist soil. The beautifully shaped leaves will also need regular cleaning.

▷ The popular Swiss cheese plant (*Monstera deliciosa*), which will thrive in most conditions.

▷ The banana tree (*Musa dwarf Cavendish*) has large dramatic leaves, making it a real statement piece. It can reach up to 3 metres in height.

▲ *The Swiss cheese plant (*Monstera deliciosa*) is one of the easiest plants to grow as it tolerates most conditions except direct sunlight.*

The quick plant guide

Easy-to-grow varieties These specimens will tolerate a certain amount of neglect, so are perfect if you are unsure about how to care for your plants or have little time on your hands.

▷ Mother-in-law's tongue (*Sansevieria*) has a strong reputation for being one of the easiest plants to care for, ideal for novice horticulturists.

▸ *An unusual and striking display of plants in glass containers but do check your plant will tolerate having its roots exposed.*

▾ *The very sculptural Staghorn fern* (Platycerium bifurcatum) *is one of the most popular house plants.*

▷ Each of the many types of cactus can tolerate being ignored for months.
▷ Aloe vera is easy to grow and propagate plus it has been used for thousands of years for its healing properties.
▷ Ivy (*Hedera helix*) keeps on growing as long as it has decent light.
▷ The Chinese money plant (*Pilea peperomioides*) is a fast grower but does require a lot of watering.
▷ The Spider plant (*Chlorophytum comosum*) will thrive almost anywhere, including bathrooms.
▷ Most air plants need no care at all and can get the water they need from the surrounding air.

The thing about plants and bathrooms Low lighting and high humidity together with sudden changes in temperature make this a tough environment for plants to thrive in. Thankfully, there are some that can handle the pressure:

▷ Ivy (*Hedera helix*) is the perfect bathroom plant. As an added benefit, one of its many amazing properties is the ability to remove mould from the surrounding air.

▷ Boston fern (*Nephrolepis exaltata*) is usually found in forests so will do well in indirect light and humid conditions.

▷ Dragon trees (*Dracaena)* love a steamy shower room.

▲ *Group all your plants together to create your own indoor garden.*

Direct sunlight Too much sunlight can often be a problem with plants, resulting in leaf scorching (when the leaves turn a brown colour at the tip). These plants have no such sensitivities:

▷ Fiddle-fig leaf (*Ficus lyrata*) is a statement piece and will do well displayed on its own.

▷ String-of-pearls (*Senecio rowleyanus*) is from the succulent family and is easy to take cuttings from.

▷ Croton (*Codiaeum variegatum*) is a tropical plant that can be a little temperamental. The key is to not overwater it. It also has the most beautiful patterned leaves.

Low light No plant will grow in complete darkness, but there are plenty of alternatives for a poorly lit area:

▷ Peace lily (*Spathiphyllum*) has stunning white blooms, and it can also thrive in a poorly lit bathroom.

▷ Bamboo (*Bambuseae*) will grow with little light or soil.

▷ The ZZ plant (*Zamioculcas zamiifolia*), the toughest house plant, needs little light or water.

▷ Ivy (*Hedera helix*) is a good trailing option.

The case for fake plants

If you really aren't the green-fingered type, there is another way to incorporate some flora into your home. In recent years there has been a complete turnaround when it comes to the once-frowned-upon world of fake plants. Nowadays you can barely tell faux from real. Designers such as Abigail Ahern are creating faux botanicals like you have never seen before, and faking it is hot in the designer world at the moment. There are also many advantages to mixing a few fakes in amongst the real thing. Obviously they require zero maintenance, but there's also the added bonus that you don't have to consider whether a plant is next to a radiator or in a room with little or no natural light.

Displaying plants

When it comes to presenting your chosen flora, the world is your oyster. Choose a vessel that will complement the plant in the same way that you pick shoes to complement an outfit. There's no need to match your pots, but they should all blend together well and have a common denominator. For example, group together white pots of different sizes, shapes and textures to create an interesting display.

▲ *When choosing houseplants always consider the amount of natural light available.*

Containers From recycled tin cans to designer pieces, there are plenty of ways to display your greens. Bohemian homes favour natural materials such as palm leaf baskets, hanging macramé holders and even wood. The humble terracotta pot is the cheapest and easiest to find in any hardware DIY store and it can easily be painted and customized, making it a perfect option for the creative types.

Also consider places like Etsy and similar marketplaces which are full of hand-thrown, unique ceramic pots that will complement an eclectic boho interior.

Arranging and grouping When grouping plants together, choose a variety of sizes, colours and textures to create depth, layer and interest. Place larger plants at the back and reserve trailing plants for shelves and hanging planters. Succulents and small plants work well on desks and tables whilst larger specimens benefit from being placed directly on the floor.

The importance of soft furnishings

It is impossible to talk about bohemian design without mentioning the abundance of textiles that feature in it. Think multi-tonal ikat, tie dye, lace, crochet, tribal prints – the possibilities are endless when it comes to layering fabrics. In true bohemian style, there is no one-size-fits-all solution. Walking into a bohemian home is not only a visual feast where no colour is off limits, but also a tactile one.

The art of layering

Unlike other styles of decor, bohemian's mantra is definitely 'more is more'. Whether you are dressing a window, a floor, a sofa or a bed, the same theory applies: layer and mix colours, patterns and most importantly textures to create interest and depth to the scheme. Heap up the cushions, choosing contrasting textures such as velvet, silk and wool. Rugs should be plentiful and usually cover most of the floor in a bohemian home. Vintage Berber, block print dhurrie, braided Chindi or rag rugs – whatever takes your fancy – pile them thick. You can also add floor pillows to create an instant casual seating area.

Repurpose

The essence of bohemian design is non-conformism and individualism. In that spirit, a lace tablecloth found in a thrift store can be hung up as a curtain. A sari from India can serve as a tablecloth or be made into cushions. Rugs can be hung on the wall and blankets can double up as curtains. There is no place here for matching bedding and curtains and it is best to search for

individual makers (on Etsy, for example) or vintage items that you can repurpose yourself. That said, some of the high street stores do sell a good selection of interesting textiles which, when mixed with a few carefully chosen individual pieces, will work just fine.

▲ *This bohemian bedroom appeals to the senses with a rich mix of fabrics and colours.*

Lighting

Lighting can make or break the ambience of a room and should be approached in the same way as any other decorating style when creating your boho home. Obviously the type and amount of natural light will determine how much artificial lighting is needed, but bohemian style favours textures. Sometimes a heavy window treatment may render a room quite dark but, used cleverly, lighting can turn dark and dingy corners into cosy and moody snugs, zoning out different areas of a room. In any case, lighting should generally be layered into three types:

▷ Ambient, the base layer – the one providing overall illumination
▷ Accent, the second layer, which highlights architectural details of a room
▷ Task, the third layer, which lights up areas of work like a desk or prep areas in the kitchen.

There is also a fourth layer rarely mentioned in lighting plans but crucial when it comes to bohemian design: candlelight.

Ambient lighting

This is your main lighting source, usually placed in the middle of the ceiling. This is your statement piece, the one you can go all-out on. Go big to create drama, from oversized rice paper lanterns to full-on glam chandeliers, which will add texture and set the tone for the rest of the room. Hang your light low and it will become the focus of the room. Fitting a dimmer switch will enable you to adjust the level of brightness and stop it looking like an interrogation room.

Bohemian statement ambient lighting This would have to be the chandelier. New and vintage, there are a huge amount of styles to choose from, from traditional crystal to the earthier clay bead contenders. They also come in a vast array of prices and sizes. Just remember: the bigger a chandelier, the bigger the statement.

◄ *Hand-painted Chinese lanterns bring an authentic touch of Far Eastern flair to any room.*

◄ *Hang several HK Living fabric lanterns in a cluster to create a focal point.*

▼ *The velvet table lamp from Madam Stoltz not only provides a soft pool of light but also adds colour and texture to the corner of the room.*

Bohemian budget ambient lighting The rice paper lantern is a great way to light up your boho home on a budget, and they come in a variety of colours and sizes. A little trick is to group a few lanterns together. Choose different sizes and hang at different heights for affordable yet statement-worthy lighting.

Bohemian textural ambient lighting Rattan, date palm, bamboo, seagrass, raffia and even reed – the emphasis here is on the organic texture of the light.

Bohemian vintage ambient light Bohemian style is all about vintage and the only advice here is to get your vintage purchase checked out by a professional before attempting to install it. Here are my top five vintage lights:

▷ Italian cocoon hanging lamp
▷ Murano glass prism chandelier
▷ Tole Pineapple chandelier
▷ Svend Aage Holm Sørensen Artichoke lamp
▷ Fun Verner Panton retro shell chandelier

Moroccan lantern These bring a touch of the exotic and are often seen in bohemian homes. When lit, they cast beautiful patterns across the room and so make the perfect ambient lighting.

Accent lighting

This type of lighting is directed towards a particular object or feature. It can draw attention to a piece of art or plants, highlight shelves or showcase displays of personal collections. Choose from a selection of recess spotlights, track lighting or picture lights, and remember that the emphasis will be on the object you wish to highlight, not the light source itself.

▲ Aside from adding gorgeous scents to your room, candles create a cosy and intimate setting.

▶ Don't feel constrained to use traditional storage. Vintage cupboards are perfect to hide anything in, from toys to linen.

Task lighting

This layer of lighting is the one most often forgotten or treated as an afterthought, but it is possibly the most important. Task lighting does exactly what the name suggests and enables you to carry out certain tasks in a particular room. It could take the form of desk lamps, anglepoise floor lamps or specific lighting for kitchens and bathrooms.

Table lamps These little light sources are your best friends and can fulfil multiple purposes within your overall lighting scheme. Table lamps can be used as ambient lighting, giving your room a soft, dappled glow. Place them on or near a reflective surface and they will also work as accent lighting. With an adequately bright lightbulb they can also fulfil the function of task lighting. However you choose to use them, table lamps will add another layer of texture, so choose rich fabrics like velvet and ramp up the statement they make with bold colours and embellishments like fringing.

Candles Despite being one of the oldest lighting sources, candles are often forgotten. This is a real shame, as they not only provide the softest light but most importantly they create a cosy, warm glow and give your room a relaxing vibe. Whether you keep them bare in a cluster or choose statement holders, they will turn any space into a welcoming sanctuary.

Choosing the right pieces

It can be hard to think in terms of practicalities when it comes to a decor style mostly led by a lack of rules to abide by. Navigating through the various needs of family life whilst still retaining the essence of boho can be a tough call. But for this style to remain eclectic rather than chaotic, it is essential to choose pieces that are right for your home, the people that reside there and the way you live.

Family life

As parents, it can be a struggle to maintain a balance between beautiful design and the practicalities of everyday life with children. Thankfully, bohemian style is a family-friendly one, and managing the chaos may be easier than you think.

Vintage furniture is your best friend Dining tables take a lot of abuse from children. Choosing a vintage piece that has already seen its fair share of knocks means you won't notice a few more scratches and it can easily be replaced once the children are older.

Choose a leather sofa Children and spillages go hand in hand, especially in the living room. To give you some piece of mind, opt for a leather sofa, which can be quickly cleaned with just soap and water. Leather is also much more hard-wearing than fabric and will more readily tolerate tumbling tots.

Storage Baskets and wooden crates are a great way to sort and store children's toys to keep the clutter at bay, plus they look perfectly at home in a bohemian house.

Flooring You can still pile on the rugs, but remember to choose ones that are washable and save the vintage ones for low-traffic areas.

Working life

More and more of us are choosing to work from home these days, and that means a lack of storage can soon become problematic. Choose vintage filing cabinets or metal lockers to store all of your work materials when not in use.

Guests

Coping with overnight guests even if you don't have a spare room is easy in a bohemian home. Sofas are often low and sectional and can easily be transformed into a temporary bed. Equally, day beds make perfect occasional seating and will fit perfectly in your boho decor scheme.

Deciding what to invest in

Pulling together any successful decorating scheme involves spending wisely and investing the bulk of your cash in items that will last for years. In a bohemian home, most of these pieces will likely be vintage or collectable antiques, but remember that whatever you choose, the number one criterion is for you to be completely in love with your purchase. Here are a few examples of items worth investing in:

Vintage and antiques

In bohemian design, this is where you should be doing most of your big spending. Yes, it is possible to buy very good replicas, but nothing can replace years of patina. Your boho home should tell a story, and pre-loved pieces of furniture can do just that. Invest in pieces you will want to keep for ever, like sideboards, tables, sofas and beds. These will become family heirlooms, no doubt treasured for years to come.

Statement lighting

Whether you choose to go vintage or brand new, lighting can often be the focal point of a room, so always buy the best you can afford. Large chandeliers are always a good choice in bohemian decor. They don't come cheap, but there are numerous places to buy good second-hand pieces. Just remember to always get lighting checked and fitted by a professional.

Art

It may seem frivolous to splurge on a beautiful piece of art, but this is where you can really let your personality shine through your bohemian home. Build a collection over time and look for new and up-and-coming artists to keep the costs down. Etsy is a wonderful place to start as they feature a huge range of independent illustrators and painters, but also many pieces of vintage art.

◄ *An oversized handmade pendant light takes pride of place over the dining room table.*

Shopping in mainstream stores

Shopping from the high street may seem like a contradiction in terms when trying to achieve an individual and personal bohemian look, but, thanks to a recent renewed interest in all things boho, it is easier than ever to bag yourself a few essentials without needing to travel the world or hunt through hundreds of charity shops. Finding a balance between new and old can be a hard one to navigate, however, as the decor needs to appear to have grown organically rather than as a result of a huge spending spree in Ikea.

To help you tread that tricky fine line, here are some dos and don'ts of shopping mainstream:

▷ **Don't** buy everything from one store. It may be tempting but unless you want your room to look like a page out of their catalogue, be selective.
▷ **Do** buy items that can be personalised. For example, belly baskets are a popular choice in boho design and are easy to find in large department stores. These can easily be customised with paint, or by adding tassels or jewels, thus transforming an ordinary purchase into something individual (see page 48 for more DIY ideas).
▷ **Do** choose timeless classic pieces such as plain linen sheets and woollen throws which will stand the test of time and not be instantly identified as a high street purchase.

▷ **Don't** buy matching anything, not even crockery.
▷ **Do** use items for a different purpose than the one intended. For example, few people use flat sheets and you can often find them on the bargain tables of department stores. These can easily be made into curtains or tablecloths or even throws. Though, saying that…
▷ **Don't** purchase something just because it is in the sale; buy it because you love it.

If you stick to those few rules, you will achieve a look that appears to have grown over years of careful thrifting. Remember, though, that the bohemian look is at its core unique and individual, and whilst furniture and accessories from high street stores can help to achieve the look, they should be used sporadically.

▶ *The Ikea two-door cupboard blends in perfectly in this eclectic room. It is ideal to store and display colourful textiles, books and candleholders.*

Adding handcrafted touches

As you might expect given the individualist, rebellious streak that runs through bohemian design, handmade, personal details are a must. And what better way to infuse your home with personality than with accessories and art that you have made yourself? Not the artistic type? Don't worry. You don't need to have graduated from art school to add handcrafted touches; there are many ways for you to let those artistic juices flow and add some creativity and individuality to your boho abode.

Personalise your walls

Unleash your artistic side and create your own wall murals. Whether it be simple geometric shapes or intricate nature scenes, this is a dramatic way to instantly inject some personality into your bohemian home. If you are not feeling brave enough to go freehand, there are many stencils available on the market, such as mandala motifs, which can be applied to your walls, floors or even furniture in a matter of minutes. Sites like Spoonflower even let you design your own wallpaper (and fabric).

Paint furniture

Repurpose old furniture by painting and adding stencils or hand-drawn designs to it. No need to spend hours sanding and prepping either. There are many good chalk paints on the market (Annie Sloan, for example) that are quick and easy to use. Feeling creative? You could even take a class to master the trickiest techniques.

DIY your own wall hangings

Wall hangings are a real staple of bohemian design. Make your own by tying pieces of twine or jute to driftwood. This really does not require much craft know-how and there are many tutorials on the web to guide you along the way. The more seasoned DIYers amongst you could even try the art of macramé.

Add trimmings

It may require a needle and thread, but one way to instantly transform your current soft furnishings is to start adding boho trimmings. Personalise your lampshades, cushions, throws – anything you like really – with brocade ribbons, pompoms or tassels. As well as adding a handcrafted touch, this is a good way to turn any plain, affordable items into jaw-dropping accessories. Marketplaces like Etsy have got a huge range of vintage and new haberdashery, too.

Personalise accessories

Baskets, mason jars, planters and containers can all be embellished with paint and/or trimmings in a matter of minutes. If you find yourself lacking in inspiration, there are hundreds of tutorials on YouTube or Pinterest and in stores like Hobbycraft.

▸ *The intricately hand-painted piano gives the room a personalised touch.*

3. A ROOM-BY-ROOM GUIDE

ENTERING

The entryway

The entryway is often the most neglected part of a house, despite it being the one that must work the hardest. Not only does it need to serve many different functions throughout the day, it also sets the tone and mood for the rest of the home, offering tantalizing glances at other rooms. It is usually a small room, often an awkward shape, and one in which form and function need to work together seamlessly.

Furniture

Choosing furniture for the hallway involves thinking aesthetically but also functionally. You could be fooled into thinking that the bohemian entryway requires little storage and that everything and anything can be displayed freely. Nothing could be further from the truth. It is clever storage solutions that will enable you to really showcase your prized possessions and conceal the ugly. Design it like you would any other room of the house: look at your lifestyle and how you and others use the space and find solutions to store the few things you wish to hide. We are not talking about applying the strict principles of the likes of Marie Kondo and other minimalist obsessives, but rather turning a cluttered space into an organized, eclectic, beautiful and personality-filled room.

Consider carefully what you wish people to see as they enter your home, but remember there are no hard-and-fast rules about how you create a show-stopping entryway. A large collection of hats could be made into a wall display; a glass-fronted cabinet might showcase an ever-growing stash of shoes; whilst your obsession for vintage clothing could be displayed on a simple makeshift driftwood hanging rail for all to see. This is show-and-tell time.

▲ *A bold choice of deep red wallpaper and rug is balanced by the rich tones of the wooden staircase and parquet floor.*

▶ *Wall tiles can be a practical and unusual option in a high traffic area such as the hallway.*

Lighting

When it comes to lighting your hallway, it's important to consider multiple light sources: a ceiling light for practical, day-to-day use; accent lights over artwork; but also table lamps to create that all-important welcoming feel. Whatever choice you make, be sure to layer your lighting to create the impression of space. When it comes to choosing your pendant light, consider the height of your ceilings. If they are high, indulge in a large statement pendant such as a vintage chandelier; if they are low, perhaps choose a design that sits flush to the ceiling.

Colour

The hallway is a transient space, which makes it the ideal location for playing with colours, patterns and textures. Of course, you know by now there are no strict rules in bohemian design. However, whether you choose a bright colour or plain white, there are a few factors to consider first, such as the amount of natural light available and how much pattern and colour is used in the display of personal collections. Nevertheless, the entryway is the perfect place for heavily patterned vintage wallpapers or bold and intense paint-colour choices.

▲ Positioning a mirror on one wall is a good trick as it will bounce the light around and help make the space feel larger. It's also useful in enabling you to check your appearance before leaving the house.

Individual, one-off vintage pieces are preferable and will give the room character. If the hallway is spacious enough, the addition of a sideboard or vintage lockers may be the perfect storage solution; if not, baskets and vintage crates are a good alternative.

Another popular addition to bohemian hallways is a bench or a chair – somewhere to sit whilst removing your shoes or on which to display cushions, throws, shopping baskets, a collection of books or even a piece of artwork.

Finishing touches

Whether you choose to add drama to the walls with dark, inky hues or strip everything back to show off distressed bare plaster, there are plenty of ways to add more colour, texture and interest to your hallway.

Mirrors are one of the most commonly used accessories in an entryway. They will bounce light around the room, create an illusion of space and add instant charm. Whether you choose a simple cluster of frameless vintage mirrors hung with sari ties or a more flamboyant sunburst mirror, they will help the room feel more open and spacious.

Hallways make great places for hanging art and will give visitors a glimpse of what's in store for the rest of the house. Think prints and original paintings, but also more textural macramé wall hangings, an intricately embroidered Suzani or perhaps a mud cloth tapestry.

Just like any other room in the house, plants feature heavily in bohemian entrance halls, so don't forget to include them here too. If your hallway is lacking in natural light, then opt for faux plants or choose specimens requiring very little light to thrive (see page 38 for a more detailed guide on which plants do well in these conditions).

Finally, pay particular attention to your floor coverings. Tiled and wooden floors are usually the most practical choice in a high-traffic area and can be accessorized with layers of vintage rugs, providing texture and a wonderful tactile experience.

◄ *A bench or low table is the perfect perch to take shoes on and off.*

Case study

Designer/Owner Roze de Witte and Pierre Traversier > **Year(s)** 2016 > **Place** Portinax, Ibiza

Often a neglected part of the home, the hallway can be tricky to plan, especially if space is limited. This hallway, however, is a perfect example of how welcoming the space can be. Plants, as we know, feature heavily in every bohemian home and are especially useful in a hallway, where they can be used effectively to hide all manner of clutter. Here, by cleverly interspersing greenery alongside essential day-to-day items, the eye is immediately drawn away from the unsightly boots and shoes in favour of the lush plant life. Trailing succulents, suspended here from the ceiling in rustic pot holders, soften the hard tile and concrete backdrop. You could hang these on anything from a peg rail to a hook, nail or coat rack for an effective yet inexpensive way to furnish a small entryway. To complete the earthy look, the wooden shelving and stool blend in and provide an interesting textural contrast. The addition of a small armchair not only provides somewhere to sit and put your shoes on, but adds to the lived-in feel of this room, which exudes a relaxed, non-precious vibe.

Bohemian Style at Home

Plants *The plants you choose will depend on the amount of light available so choose carefully.*

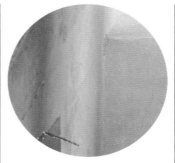

Colour *Although the walls are not painted, the predominant colour is green, a colour associated with nature and a stress-relieving, calming colour perfect for a hallway.*

Hanging plant holders *Hanging plant holders are easily available from stores or you could make your own simplified version like here.*

Wooden floor *Wooden floors are often the preferred option combining warmth with practicality.*

Seating *If you have room, an armchair will help to make the hallway a welcoming place.*

Display *Green glass bottles are a clever way to bring more colour and texture into a small space.*

Signature colours

Brown isn't present on the colour wheel, and is possibly one the most overlooked and undervalued colours when it comes to decorating. Bohemian homes have an inextricable connection with nature, which makes brown hues particularly welcome, since they bring a grounded earthiness to the decor scheme.

We are more familiar with brown as a texture, as it usually features heavily in most houses in the form of wooden furniture and floorboards. When it comes to choosing a paint colour, however, brown still has a bad rap, and is often branded a boring choice. This is a shame, to say the least, since it is a very versatile neutral, with the biggest variety of shades available. From caramel to dark chocolate, browns create a cosy vibe with their earthy, rich tones such as the fawny brown walls of this hallway.

Upon entering, the eyes are immediately drawn to the striking blue-and-white painted floorboards. White paint here would have made the space too stark and clinical, while the earthiness of the brown walls warms the space and welcomes you in, making you feel safe and comfortable. The soft mustard yellow on the door frame and skirting boards complements and lifts the brown without being overbearing. Finally, the muted tones of the paintings pull the whole colour scheme together – a scheme that is peaceful and easy on the eye but not dull or boring with such a bold choice of flooring.

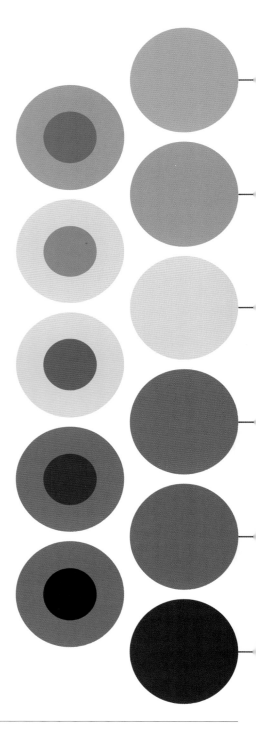

Mid-century frameless mirror

Mirrors not only reflect us but also their surroundings, and in that sense can totally transform a room, bringing light and a sense of space to even the darkest, dingiest areas of the house. Busy bohemian homes often favour the simple style of mid-century mirrors, which offer an abundance of history and patina at an affordable price.

Those mirrors, like many mid-century pieces, are all about form and function. The function, of course, is simple, but when it comes to the form, there is a huge variety of shapes to choose from. Whether streamlined or sculptured, famous producers to look out for include the likes of Artemide, Luxus, Pedersen & Hansen and Kalmar, to name but a few.

The beautiful eight-sided vintage wall mirror opposite features a simple bevelled edge and still has its original backing. It has a linked-metal hanging chain and could be displayed alongside others in a cluster or as a standalone piece in a hallway, bedroom or bathroom to add charm and character.

Source
Owl and the Elephant
owlandtheelephant.co.uk

Material
Glass, metal

Dimensions
Width: 37 cm
Height: 67 cm

Macramé wall hanging

Macramé is an ancient craft dating as far back as the 13th century. The first known macramé weavers were Arabic, who began tying decorative knots to secure the loose ends of woven textiles like towels and shawls. The most prolific and influential weavers, though, were sailors.

Macramé has had its fair share of falling in and out of fashion over the years. During the Victorian era, it was all the rage, and could be found adorning everything from bedspreads to tablecloths. Its popularity then died down, only to resurface with a vengeance alongside hippie culture during the 1970s. Everything from bikinis to bedding – even the humble toilet-roll holder – was made from macramé. Over the past five years, the craft has once again been making a comeback to grace many a texture-loving interior.

The 'Fleur' macramé wall hanging opposite is an incredibly detailed piece – beautifully textured; strong and solid in its presence and the perfect statement piece for a bohemian home. Made from no less than five layers of intricately hand-knotted pure natural Australian cotton, it hangs on a naturally fallen branch. Each creation is authentic and unique in style and many hours are invested in making a single piece this size.

Source
Round Nine
roundnine9.com

Material
100% natural Australian cotton

Dimensions
Height: 120 cm
Width: 52 cm

Naga chair

The Naga people are a group of tribes inhabiting the Naga Hills of the Nagaland state in north-eastern India. Infamous for being fierce head-hunters, the tribe has a rich tradition of art and craft rooted in a lifestyle that is in complete harmony with their environment, creating their own colourful clothing, jewellery, headgear and skilfully producing wood carvings, metal-work, weaving, basketry and pottery.

The Naga chair opposite is hand-carved from a single piece of wood. Its organic, ethnic and primitive design would make the ideal addition to the bohemian hallway, perfect to perch on whilst taking off shoes.

Source
Couleur locale
couleurlocale.eu

Material
Wood

Dimensions
Height: 100 cm
Width: 40 cm
Seat height: 40 cm

Boujad rug

Bohemian homes are filled with rugs, not only on the floors but also serving as wall hangings and even sofa and seat covers. Old and vintage examples like the Boujad rug opposite are preferred to those that are new and uniform, as they will not only add texture and layers, but history and character to the bohemian interior.

Boujad rugs are hand-woven pile rugs made in and around the town of Boujad in the Middle Atlas Mountains of Morocco. Diverse in composition and weave, each Boujad is unique. The woven patterns are often symbolic – imagined by each weaver and telling a tale with the use of traditional Berber motifs, making references to fertility, marriage and spiritual beliefs. They are regarded as works of art and feature playful use of bold colours like oranges, pinks, reds and greens.

Source
Vinterior
vinterior.co.uk

Material
Knotted wool

Dimensions
Length: 220 cm
Width: 140 cm

Banjara wall hanging

The Banjara are a tribal people from India. Due to their nomadic lifestyle, they primarily earn their living as labourers rather than farmers. However, the growing interest in their bold, distinctive embroideries has given them an alternate source of income.

Handed down from generation to generation, Banjara designs are strikingly different to those of other tribes and are mostly very colourful. The Banjara hand-stitch their fabrics using different patterns, colourful threads and remnants of textiles, and one also finds coins, cowrie shells, buttons or mirrors in their work, and this is what makes these embroideries stand apart from the rest. Increasing demand from the Western world for their vintage tapestry wall art, bedspreads and cushions has thankfully helped to keep this traditional craft alive.

The wall hanging opposite is mostly cream and features a multitude of bright and colourful embroidery. It could also be used as a bedspread, a throw or even a door curtain.

Source
Homevestures
homevestures.com

Material
Mixed

Dimensions
Height: 163 cm
Width: 78 cm

RELAXING

The living room

Usually the largest room of the house, the living room is the place to entertain guests and relax with the family. In a bohemian home, it is the most welcoming of spaces, and is usually centred around a comfortable seating arrangement. It may also have a fireplace to ramp up the cosiness and will be rich in textures and art. Whilst a television may be present, it will rarely be the focus of the room. Everything in this space, from the art to the furniture, focuses on comfort and contributes to its calm, easy-going feel.

The seating

The seating arrangement in bohemian homes is rarely a formal affair. Low seating is often the preferred choice, as well as floor seating and the occasional chair. A good option seen in many bohemian living rooms is a versatile sectional sofa, such as the Togo from Ligne Roset or the Anfibio by Alessandro Becchi. Whatever you choose, it will almost certainly be vintage and above all comfortable. The bohemian living room is a social one and caters very well for extra guests dropping in unexpectedly. Floor cushions scattered on deep pile rugs will provide instant seating for those occasions. The addition of other non-matching chairs, such as the rattan peacock or a leather butterfly, provides more places to relax as well as a mix of interesting textures and materials.

▲ *Add interest to plain walls with a gallery wall that reflects the colours of the room.*

▶ *The surfboard makes the space a personal one and gives visitors a glimpse into the owner's lifestyle.*

Soft furnishings

The main characteristic of a bohemian living room is its tactile appeal. It should stimulate all the senses whilst enabling you to unwind. The richness and variety of textiles is a bohemian home's trademark. Cushions embellished with appliqué and fringing as well as woven throws and rugs will be plentiful and varied. To achieve the richness of

the look, you will need to contrast textures and mix fabrics like velvet, linen and cotton and then combine as many prints and colours as you see fit. Vintage Moroccan rugs are a popular choice in bohemian design and it is common practice to layer multiple rugs one on top of the other to create a space exuding pure comfort and relaxation.

Greenery

We must never forget the importance of plants in the bohemian home, and the living room in particular can sometimes resemble a mini jungle. Play with scale and mix a wide variety of sizes. Don't forget to vary the colour of the plants as well

as the shape and size of the leaves. Place them on the floor, on side tables and windowsills. You could even hang them from the ceiling. There are never too many plants in a bohemian living room.

Art and personal collections

The bohemian home is a treasure trove of eclectic art and varied personal items. Whatever you choose to display, remember that it should always tell the story of who you are and what you value. So, if you enjoy reading, you could display your books – not just on book shelves, but also on coffee tables and even stacked up on the floor. You could make the display even more personal by framing your favourite page from a book. If you enjoy travelling, showcase any maps of places you have been alongside any trinkets you have brought back from these exotic locations. Display a beautiful item of clothing by simply hanging it on the wall, and don't be afraid to show off your children's colourful artwork either. Remember: anything and everything you treasure can be the object of a display.

Lighting

Creating a space in which to relax involves choosing good lighting. Overhead pendant lights can be used as a focal point, but you will also need some kinder, softer lighting such as table lamps to bring texture to this aspect of the decor too. There is not one particular must-have designer light in bohemian design, but large chandeliers are a common option. Hang them low over a coffee table for added effect and drama. Another popular choice is mid-century lighting, or even the bold and glamorous 1970s pendants. Mixing eras and styles will give your bohemian living room an eclectic and worldly atmosphere. Candles are often overlooked

◄ Express your personality by painting your own piece of abstract art to reflect the colours used in the room.

◄◄ Plants can add another layer of colour to the living room.

when planning a lighting scheme, and they not only provide the kindest, softest glow, but can also evoke memories of forgotten places through their scents.

Colour

Thinking about bohemian living rooms conjures up ideas of vividly bright and clashing colours, but it is useful to remember that with a style that prides itself on its lack of rules, it is common for the colours to be less important than the textures and patterns employed. Earthier, somewhat muted colours are now emerging in the bohemian decor scheme, with just a few splashes of more vivid tones. The walls are sometimes left white to really highlight the different pops of colours found on the soft furnishings and accessories. For an alternative to paint, vintage floral wallpapers can create a nostalgic feel in your living room.

Case study

Designer/Owner Jo Brittles > **Year(s)** 2018 > **Place** Gold Coast, Australia

The bohemian living room is above all a social one. It says, 'Come on in; kick off your shoes and stay awhile.' This is a space bursting with personality, providing a real feast for the senses.

The key here was to create a room that appears to have evolved organically rather than one that looks to have been carefully thought out. From the vintage kilim cushions to the Tretchikoff print casually resting on the hand-painted sideboard, every item has a history that intensifies the overall eclectic look. In true bohemian style, this space appears to have been furnished as a result of years of careful thrifting. The owner gave a nod to the 1970s too, with the iconic rattan peacock chair, which works well with the abundance of plants and greenery.

The interplay of brightly coloured pillows and patterned throws is typical of the boho look. The white walls are soothing against such bold textiles and draw attention to the unusual art on display, where the emphasis is on texture rather than colour.

The Moroccan pouffes strewed across the antique rug provide additional seating and add to the overall relaxed vibe of this room.

Cushions *More is more when it comes to cushions. Just be sure to vary pattern, colour and texture.*

Painted sideboard *This is a perfect example of how to inject personality into your home, and painted pieces like this one are a great way to upcycle old furniture.*

Art *Art is a great way to add personality to your walls. Vladimir Tretchikoff's prints are a favourite in bohemian homes.*

Plants *Plants add an extra layer of texture and colour. If you don't have a green thumb, then choose the fake variety.*

Throw *Vintage Suzanis are one-of-a-kind pieces of art. With their intricate embroideries, they can be used as wall hangings or throws and are a great way to bring colour into a room.*

Floor cushions *Floor cushions are very versatile accessories which can be used as footstools, low tables or to provide extra seating.*

Signature colours

Bright colours in a room needn't be reserved just for the walls. This statement-worthy multicoloured sofa packs a punch, working in contrast with the plain white walls to form an intense and passionate colour palette. The audacious combination of vintage Suzani fabric with purple velvet on a single piece of furniture immediately draws the eye, creating a focal point for the room.

Suzanis are made using bright, vibrant colours in floral and medallion patterns and never fail to create a bold and dramatic impact. When contrasting complementary colours, however, it is important to remember that, for the scheme to retain balance, not all colours should be used in equal amounts. Here, the two dominant colours in the room are purple and yellow, accented by hues of red, orange, pink, green and blue. Despite sitting opposite each other on the colour wheel, purple and yellow really do complement and enhance one another, and although at first glance it seems to be a veritable riot of colour, there is in fact a tight palette on display here. The playful and exuberant yellow rug intensifies and deepens the purple of the sofa, while the traditional gallery wall has been replaced by an eclectic display of necklaces, repeating all the colours in the sofa as well as adding that all-important personal touch. Finally, greenery is always a powerful tool in your bohemian design arsenal, adding colour, shape and life to the room.

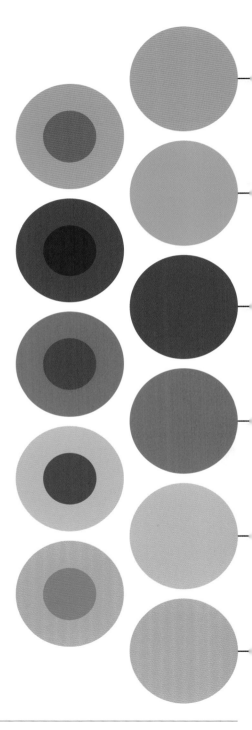

Leather pouffe

The pouffe is a piece of furniture used as a footstool or low seat. It is distinguished from a stool in that it is completely covered in cloth or leather with no feet or legs visible and is essentially a large hard cushion. It is easy to see why Bohemian homes have embraced the versatile Moroccan version of the humble pouffe, adding an ethnic feel to the room whilst providing extra seating for guests. You can even pop a tray on top to transform it into an instant dining area—it is a very useful multifunctional piece of furniture.

This dark brown oiled pouffe is crafted from leather and dyed. Traditionally adorned with Moroccan patterns, it is embroidered with either cotton or silk and hand-stitched by local artisans in Morocco.

Source
Bohemia Design
bohemiadesign.co.uk

Material
Leather

Dimensions
Height: 32 cm
Diameter: 53 cm

Glass chandelier

There are many light fixtures associated with bohemian design, but none bring such a strong sense of theatrical drama to a room as the glass chandelier. Steeped in history, it takes us right back to the beginnings of boho, as far back as 16th-century Bohemia (now known as the Czech Republic). Home to the world's first glass factory, the city soon became the world's leading manufacturer of glass, also known as Bohemian crystal. The first Bohemian chandeliers were created by glass cutter Josef Palme in 1724.

When it comes to sourcing a glass chandelier for your own home, there are a multitude of designs, shapes and sizes to choose from. Most are made from brass, bronze or crystal and are sometimes adorned with glass beads. Nowadays, while it is still possible to find glass crystal chandeliers, several more affordable options are available, such as those that use wood or clay beads or are made entirely from shell and even paper. This staple of bohemian design can be purchased new or second-hand from all kinds of sources.

The three-tier Eve chandelier opposite features crystallized glass pendants hung from an aged bronze frame and bears all the characteristics of a vintage piece. The understated design evokes times past and maximizes the boho vibes, adding a touch of glamour to an otherwise relaxed decor without being gaudy. It gives the room another layer of texture and an otherworldly dimension that is typical of bohemian design.

Source
Venice Beach House
venicebeachhouse.co.uk

Materials
Crystallized glass, bronze

Dimensions
Height: 24 cm
Depth: 29 cm

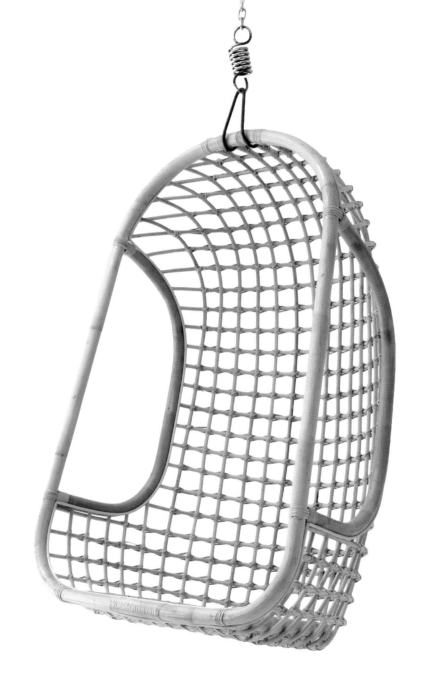

Hanging chair

The popular hanging egg chair was created in 1959 by Danish furniture designer Nanna Ditzel, whose reputation for innovative design won her a career spanning over six decades. Made from rattan in a period when skilled wicker makers and architects crafted beautifully sculptured furniture out of the challenging material, this chair remains just as desirable today as it was then.

There are very few original vintage chairs remaining, so if you are lucky enough to source one then you will usually need to be willing to pay a high price for it. Due to the popularity of all things rattan and wicker, however, it's no surprise that we are now seeing the distinctly unique style of the hanging egg chair being replicated and tweaked by many contemporary furniture designers.

A firm favourite of bohemian design, it can be paired with sheepskins, cushions and cosy throws to provide the perfect place to relax and lounge in, whether inside or outside.

Source
House Curious
housecurious.co.uk

Material
Rattan

Dimensions
Height: 110 cm
Width: 72 cm
Depth: 55 cm

Floor cushion

A bohemian living room is rich in layers of textured and colourful textiles. Piles of pillows are scattered on sofas and floors to ensure maximum comfort everywhere. Floor cushions feature heavily where they act as a stand-alone piece of furniture. They are not only a great way to accommodate extra guests but also ideal for a reading nook, a meditation corner or even an impromptu casual dinner.

This Berber floor cushion has been made from refashioned vintage Azilal rugs. There are several tribes originating from the Middle Atlas Mountains of Morocco, each with its own individual weaving style. The Azilal region uses copious amounts of colour and their hand-woven woollen rugs feature geometric and abstract designs, each of which is woven freehand.

Source
Dar Beida Moroccan Living
darbeida.com

Material
Wool, Cotton

Dimensions
Length: 55 cm
Width: 55 cm

Bohemian Style at Home

Togo sofa

It would be hard to find a more iconic piece of
1970s furniture than the Togo sofa, designed by
Michel Ducaroy for Ligne Roset. Having sold more
than 1.2 million pieces in 72 countries, the Togo's
wonderfully weird sectional design and low height
makes it perfect for laid-back bohemian homes.

When it first made its debut at the Salon des
Arts Ménagers at the Palais de la Défense, Paris,
in 1973, its crumpled, 'newborn' appearance and
Shar Pei wrinkles earned it more than a few
doubtful looks from professionals and members
of the public alike. Nevertheless, this cult piece of
the 1970s is still enjoying undiminished success
today and ranks amongst the Ligne Roset brand's
bestsellers. A bête de mode for 40 years, it has
turned up everywhere – from the lobby of the
Standard Hotel in Hollywood to Lenny Kravitz's
Paris mansion.

Source
Ligne Roset
ligne-roset.com

Vintage model shown from
Bestwelhip.nl

Material
Polyether foam

Dimensions

Seat element
Height: 70 cm
Width: 131 cm
Depth: 102 cm

Corner section
Height: 70 cm
Width: 102 cm
Depth: 102 cm

Moroccan tray table

Traditionally used to serve tea to guests in Moroccan homes, the tray table is a popular choice amongst bohemian aficionados. Its handcrafted, ethnic and multifunctional design is perfectly suited to the ultra-social boho household. A practical addition to many rooms, it makes the perfect side table in the hallway or bedside table in the bedroom. It can also double up as a casual dining table – just scatter some pillows around it to serve as impromptu chairs.

Many variants of this design are produced, but the Kasbah Moroccan tray table opposite, with its hand-engraved aluminium tray, is a fine lesson in craftsmanship. Its wooden painted legs are foldable too, which makes it easy to move and store away.

Source
India May Home
indiamayhome.co.uk

Materials
Aluminium, wood

Dimensions
Height: 49 cm
Diameter: 76 cm

COOKING

The kitchen

The bohemian kitchen isn't just a place to prepare food; it is a gathering place – somewhere we eat, entertain, work and relax. It must therefore be functional and practical as well as aesthetically pleasing, from the cupboards right down to the crockery. Unlike other rooms of the house, the kitchen also needs to accommodate a large number of unsightly electrical goods, such as a fridge, a cooker, a dishwasher, a kettle and a toaster. But, with careful thought and planning, the bohemian kitchen can be a space you will want to spend time in, where you linger with a cup of coffee and catch up with friends as well as prepare meals for the family. In this relaxed atmosphere, the bohemian cook will enjoy experimenting with new recipes, baking bread or recreating exotic dishes from places they have visited.

The furniture

There is nothing sleek, utilitarian or streamlined about a bohemian kitchen. Like the rest of the house, the kitchen is crammed with all kinds of paraphernalia, hand-me-downs and mismatched crockery. The furniture in a boho kitchen is often free-standing and vintage, but shunning traditional fitted units is not for everyone, and if you prefer the idea of fitted cabinetry you can always replace the traditional eye-level cabinets with reclaimed timber shelving. Not only will shelves help to enhance the feeling of space, they are perfect for displaying all manner of glassware and china and make for a personality-filled kitchen. To compensate for the lack of work surface, introduce a butcher's block, kitchen island or, if space permits, a large table to fulfil this function. When it comes to shopping for kitchen furniture, it pays to think outside the box. Old school cupboards, vintage armoires, an old-fashioned meat safe, glass-fronted cupboards

▲ *Add a practical and colourful touch to the kitchen window with the addition of a retro plastic fly curtain.*

▶ *A farmhouse sink can be easily fitted on top of free-standing kitchen units.*

or even old filing cabinets can all be repurposed to store food, baking utensils or bulky saucepans. A Belfast sink is a popular choice that suits the non-fitted bohemian kitchen.

Appliances

It goes without saying that a free-standing kitchen will need free-standing appliances. If budget allows, opt for an Aga, which will add instant character to the space and keep you warm and cosy in winter. Alternatively, choose from the huge array of free-standing range cookers on offer. And whilst it may not be practical to opt for vintage

appliances, replica fridges, toasters and kettles are all readily available nowadays, allowing you to instil a nostalgic feel to the kitchen without any worries about faulty connections or old-school wiring. Modern washing machines and dishwashers can easily be concealed behind a homemade curtain.

Flooring

Kitchen flooring should be practical – preferably vintage tiles or floorboards – though like any other room in a bohemian home it will more often than not be covered in rugs. Since they are more likely to take on stains here, choose inexpensive rag rugs or one of the many machine-washable options.

Lighting

The kitchen is the room that needs the most careful consideration when it comes to lighting. As a multifunctional space, the lighting must cater for various tasks, such as food preparation, eating, entertaining and even working, and you will need to layer practical and task lighting. A statement pendant light can be hung over the table and there are many available options that are suitable for a bohemian kitchen. A vintage enamel shade may be a practical choice, whilst rattan pendants cast a softer glow – perfect for entertaining friends. Consider replacing the strip lighting traditionally fixed under the wall-mounted units with some vintage Anglepoise lamps placed on the display shelves.

Display

In a bohemian home, crockery and kitchen paraphernalia will most certainly be on display. Here you can truly indulge in your maximalist tendencies and scour flea markets, car boot sales and junk shops to create an eclectic collection of

serveware, dinnerware and accessories. Vintage pieces such as coffee grinders, commercial scales, thermometers, old chopping boards and coloured glass are easy to come by and can all take pride of place in the bohemian kitchen. Store your fruit and vegetables in old crates, shopping or fishing baskets. Enamelware popular in the 1930s is so durable that there are many pieces still to be found in second-hand shops. Mismatched storage tins, kettles, coffee pots and colanders are all useful and look beautiful displayed on a shelf.

▲ Glass cabinets and open shelving enable you to display all your pretty kitchenware.

◀ Vintage tiles bring both pattern and extra colour to the kitchen.

Colour

The best foil to showcase your collection of colourful vintage kitchenware is probably white. Anything bolder and you may run the risk of overpowering your display. If you find this too sterile, however, you could always add colour or even wallpaper near the table end of the room in order to demarcate a dining area.

Plants

As we know, plants are a must in the bohemian home. In the kitchen, why not substitute herbs? Not only are they really easy to grow if you have some natural light, they will add fantastic flavour to your food as well as that all-important touch of the great outdoors. Plants and herbs in old terracotta pots placed inside a wooden crate make for a wonderful display on a windowsill.

Case study

Designer Abigail Ahern > **Year(s)** 2016 > **Place** London, UK

With every element pointing to the classic design ethics of an eclectic, bohemian-styled room, this kitchen fully embodies its role as the heart of the home. Far from cold and clinical, it is cosy, comfortable and cocoon-like, where cooking and socialising happen comfortably side by side.

It feels both seductive and intriguing – not adjectives you'd usually use to describe a kitchen! This is achieved by layering textures, warm hues and by adding elements traditionally seen in other rooms of the house, such as the use of rugs on the floor and the addition of free-standing furniture like the decorative console in front of the window displaying fruit bowls and heaps of plants. Even the lighting is warm and layered, with a mix of recessed lighting, table lamps and a very sculptural and statement-worthy chandelier, perfect for creating different moods for different occasions.

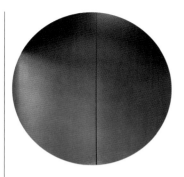

Table lighting *The oversize table lamp provides soft mood lighting as well as creating textural interest with its very tactile palm fibre shade.*

Plants *Plants are the ultimate addition to any bohemian room. For the kitchen, think of introducing herbs too.*

Colour *The choice of darker hues in the kitchen creates a more intimate and cosier feel.*

Chandelier *The chandelier provides an unusual and eye-catching lighting source for the kitchen island.*

Console *The introduction of a free-standing vintage sideboard breaks the monotony of fitted kitchen units and gives you somewhere to display plants and ornaments.*

Seating *If space allows, the addition of chairs or bar stools encourages people to linger in the kitchen.*

Signature colours

It can be hard to put into words what constitutes a bohemian room, as a lot of it has to do with the feel and the soulful qualities of the space. In this kitchen however, the designer has captured the essence of bohemian design perfectly. As well as its beautiful mix of rich colours – green metro tiles, original wood floors, a textured dusky pink wall and green ceiling – there is a clever combination of traditional fitted units and bespoke elements such as the open shelving, which allows for an artistic display of crockery and kitchenalia.

The handmade kitchen has been painted in Clerkenwell blue, which is almost a teal blue. Painting kitchen cabinetry is an easy and inexpensive way to add colour, warmth and personality to an otherwise bland, run-of-the-mill kitchen. The wood-burning stove and extravagant choice of lighting fixture transforms the room into a cosy and relaxed space in which to cook and socialize. The striking green metro tiles, inspired by the green tiles installed in the London Underground, create a strong visual focal point, adding texture and providing contrast to the soft pink walls.

The boho look is all about mixing, never matching, expressing personality and creating spaces which are practical but rule-breaking, fun and full of character. This room excels in all those aspects.

Kitchen larder cupboard

As we have seen, the bohemian kitchen is very often free-standing in form and features a mishmash collection of vintage cupboards, giving the room its signature eclectic look.

This impressively large double cupboard would have probably been originally used to store clothes and linen in the bedroom, but could just as well function as a free-standing larder in the kitchen. It has a beautifully distressed blue and navy surface finish and shows years of deep patina, giving it that true rustic aesthetic of times past. Its two doors open to reveal its teak construction and ample internal storage space for food or crockery.

Source
Scaramanga
scaramangashop.co.uk

Material
Wood

Dimensions
Height: 172 cm
Width: 125 cm

Apron sink

The apron sink, also known as a farmhouse sink, dates back to the early 17th century, when people had to haul water from wells and rivers. These early sinks were mostly found in rural homes and were not connected to a plumbing system, so needed to be filled and drained manually. Designed for comfort in a time when women spent substantial amounts of time washing up and cleaning, the exposed front of the sink allows for more internal basin space to accommodate large pots and pans.

Nowadays, the apron sink is a statement piece that adds a touch of that nostalgic, old farmhouse charm to today's modern kitchens. They can either be fitted on top of a standard kitchen cabinet or they can be free-standing, making them an ideal choice for the bohemian kitchen. The Ikea sink opposite is an affordable version of the farmhouse sink, as vintage ones can be rather costly.

Source
Ikea
Ikea.co.uk

Material
White porcelain

Dimensions
Length: 82 cm
Width: 48 cm
Depth: 48 cm

Le Creuset cocotte

Le Creuset was founded by two Belgian industrialists, Armand Desaegher and Octave Aubecq, in 1925. Their first porcelain-enamelled cast-iron pots were created at their foundry in Fresnoy-le-Grand, France, and it is from there that Le Creuset continues to produce its world-famous cookware items, which are today sold in more than 60 countries worldwide.

The process of fabrication is a long and laborious one, taking up to 120 hours to create a single item. Every Le Creuset piece is individually cast in a sand mould which is broken after use, meaning each pot is truly unique. After casting, the pots receive multiple layers of strong, chip-resistant enamel, and this process not only gives Le Creuset its individual and characteristic beauty, but creates a tough, non-reactive surface.

The cocotte, or French oven, was one of the very first items produced by Le Creuset and is still their most popular product. It's available in a large range of colours, including the iconic volcanic orange opposite.

Source
Le Creuset
lecreuset.com

Material
Cast iron, enamel

Dimensions
Varied

Kitchen table

Whether you opt for a fitted or free-standing kitchen, the room often features a central island, which serves as a great place to prep food or eat dinner. A table is a great way to incorporate a workspace that seamlessly switches over to a dining space, but also enables people to face one another instead of the cook, which provides a more sociable type of gathering than most islands can muster.

The uniquely crafted table opposite is the perfect addition to the bohemian kitchen. Made from sturdy hardwood and naturally distressed by years of use, it will bring character as well as functionality to the room. Its fold-down design allows it to be easily moved outside in the summer, making it a versatile, indispensable piece.

Source
Scaramanga
scaramangashop.co.uk

Material
Hardwood

Dimensions
Length: 178 cm
Width: 85 cm
Height: 79 cm

Kilim rug

Moroccan Berber tribes create an astonishing array of different types of rugs using 'flat weave' techniques, such as kilims, blankets and woven floor coverings that don't have a thick knotted pile. With distinctive designs that arise from the way they were woven, and which are often based on ordered geometric shapes or simple harmonious bands of colour, these rugs bring an inherently bohemian vibe to a room.

As with thick-pile rugs such as Beni Ourain, different Moroccan tribes have different weaving traditions; some use natural dyes such as henna, while others use bold red, magenta, mauve, rose, tangerine and brown hues. Regional differences abound. For example, kilims woven in the warm south of Morocco make abundant use of sunny yellow and saffron colours, hues not seen so much in the north. Motifs and symbols differ by region, too, and can represent fertility, motherhood, immortality and marriage, to name but a few.

The kilim rug opposite is a beautifully versatile vintage textile, most likely from the 1970s or 1980s. As well as being used as a soft kilim for the floor, it could also become a wall hanging or even a simple throw. Contrasting distinct Berber symbols with alternative stripes and bands, its soft palette of pastel and primary hues has been woven in wool and cotton.

Source
Maroc Tribal
maroctribal.com

Material
Wool, cotton

Dimensions
Height: 185 cm
Width: 137 cm

Kitchen shelf

The kitchen storage rack is an old item of domestic furniture and remains true to its original form, when it would display merely a few pewter plates in a sparse and functional kitchen. Nowadays, there are many variations of the plate rack and both new and vintage examples can be easily sourced.

As we know, bohemian kitchens are often free-standing affairs, giving the room a warm, welcoming and whimsical ambience. The open shelf allows for an artistic display of mismatched crockery, boot sale kitchenalia and antique cooking implements and is yet another way for the boho storyteller to showcase another collection in an unusual, non-precious way.

The distressed wooden kitchen storage rack opposite is made from a teak frame in which plates can be placed vertically. With an additional shelf for placing cups and bowls, it is strong and durable. As well as providing extra storage, it's perfect for displaying your everyday kitchen wares.

Source
Scaramanga
scaramangashop.co.uk

Material
Teak

Dimensions
Height: 74 cm
Width: 74 cm
Depth: 47 cm

EATING

The dining room

The bohemian dining room is not a formal affair; instead it's a casual, welcoming space where conversation flows and people linger till the early hours of the morning. It isn't always a separate room either – the no-rules approach to boho design allows you to set up a dining area pretty much anywhere, indoors or outdoors, giving you plenty of ways to be creative. Perhaps what most defines the bohemian dining room is its effortless, relaxed and cosy feel, where the focus lies on the company, not on any specific designer dining set.

Table

Wood is always a preferred element in bohemian design, boosting the earthy feel and adding textual variation to the room. When it comes to choosing the right dining table, many options are available. It is important to consider the shape and size of your room before deciding on the shape of the table. Rectangular tables can accommodate more guests whereas round tables are more suited to smaller rooms, creating a more intimate setting. Bohemian dining rooms have the advantage of versatility, as well as the ability to accommodate furniture from different periods. From mid-century to older antiques, no style is out of bounds, though since bohemian style is all about playing on contrasts and diversity, a simple wooden table often works beautifully when offset by a luxurious chandelier, colourful textiles or opulent table settings. Bohemian style is all about playing with contrasts and diversity. Try to choose a pre-loved piece that is imbued with history (even if you have just purchased it on eBay and have no idea what its history is!).

▲ A low table and floor cushions play host to a colourful selection of tableware for a casual dining experience.

▶ This dining room is part of a bigger open-plan room. A large rug and a tight colour palette separate this area from the rest of the space.

▲ *The long, rustic dining table has been chosen to suit the shape of the space available and make the most of the garden view.*

Chairs

Mismatched chairs are often the preferred choice for the eclectic boho home. To retain cohesion in the room, either choose the same chair in a variety of different colours or choose a combination of different styles and eras in just one shade. Another option would be to choose one unifying material, for example bamboo, and vary the shape and style. You can also team up chairs with vintage benches or rustic stools.

Storage

The classic mid-century sideboard is often seen in Bohemian dining rooms. Not only does it serve the useful purpose of storage, it is also the perfect platform on which to display your most treasured possessions. If you have space, consider choosing something a little larger, such as an armoire or a glass-fronted display cupboard. All these options can be sourced relatively inexpensively second-hand and via online auction sites.

Lighting

Dining room lighting can be tricky to get right and since the room is mostly used in the evenings, the light needs to be warm and inviting but not too dim. Flawless lighting here will create a soft, laid-back ambiance, perfect for having dinner and entertaining guests. Pendant lights will help define the look of a space and, if hung low, can also act as the table's centrepiece. A good choice might be an oversized wicker pendant or the bird's nest pendant by Ay illuminate, both of which would give your room a cosy and relaxed atmosphere. If you love vintage, then the Achille & Pier Giacomo Castiglioni cocoon light would be the perfect statement piece above the table.

Colour

Bohemian decor conjures up images of bright colours and bold hues, and the dining room is a perfect place to indulge in those rich tones, giving the room a cosy and comforting feel. As this is a less frequently used room, feel free to paint the walls in a more daring colour or even hang vintage-style wallpaper to add charm. If you opt for a more neutral base, then ramp up the colour in the curtains, rugs and accessories. Whether you choose bright colours or neutrals, the dining room should be oozing with earthiness and an abundance of natural elements all flowing together to create an effortless and intriguing space.

Accessories

Although traditional boho style is a maximalist one – loud, colourful and most certainly not about empty surfaces and blank walls – the recent emergence of a more pared-back version of boho sees more neutral wall colours that are being livened up through the use of texture-heavy rugs, macramé wall hangings and bold, oversized artwork. The right accessories will add interest to your space and make for interesting dinner conversation with guests.

Botanicals are an essential part of bohemian design and the dining room is no exception. They are an affordable way to add colour, dimension and texture to the space as well as creating a sense of wellbeing. Cacti and succulents look great on the table as a centrepiece, while tall indoor plants like fiddle leaf figs and even small trees can fill up an awkward corner and provide an unexpected focal point. Get creative with planters by varying texture and colour.

▲ *Coloured glass adds a retro touch to this table setting.*

Case study

Designer/Owner Isabelle Dubois Dumée > **Year(s)** 2018 **Place** Dirac, France

There are generally two main types of dining room: the relaxed, open-plan kitchen/diner and the formal, separate dining room where dinner parties and lingering Sunday lunches are held. This dining room combines both, and is an unfussy and sociable space. It mixes old and new seamlessly, giving this simple bohemian dining room a casual, inviting and informal feel. The old peeling wallpaper and imperfect plaster have been left untouched, celebrating years of history with layers of textural patina. The room is lit by strings of fun, festoon globe lights instead of a more formal central pendant and is simply furnished with a large, simple table and vintage mismatched wooden chairs. From the abundant use of natural materials to the plants and even the choice of lighting, everything in the room has a strong connection to nature and epitomizes laid-back bohemian living.

Bohemian Style at Home

Glass cabinet *This is a great and practical way to display a large collection of ceramics.*

Walls *Bohemian homes love telling a story and this peeling wallpaper and textured plaster are imbued in history and nostalgia.*

Lights *Festoon lights are more often seen outside than in a dining room setting but they give the room a garden party feel.*

Plants *Plants are the ultimate bohemian accessory and in such a light-filled room, there are many suitable specimens (see p.37).*

Flooring *A rug adds warmth to this large room and introduces another textural layer.*

Chairs *For a more relaxed feel to the dining room choose mismatched vintage chairs like these.*

Signature colours

The bohemian dining room is not a formal or stuffy affair. Much like the rest of the home, it has a relaxed, laid-back feel, as well as a distinct connection with nature. Whether it is a family dinner or a casual get-together with friends, the room should reflect a sense of warmth and intimacy at all times.

We know how much colour influences our moods, and picking the right shade for a dining room can be tricky. Blue is generally thought of as a relatively cool colour on the palette, more often chosen for bathrooms than for dining rooms. However, blue can be comparatively cool or warm depending on what other colours it is paired with. Here it is teamed up with green and an abundant use of wood and natural textures, working perfectly to achieve a very serene and tranquil mood. Blue is known to mix well with many colours, and coupled with the pale green chairs it becomes part of a nature-based colour palette, which removes all feelings of stiffness and pretension from this simple dining room. None of the hues chosen here compete with one another, but instead work to emphasize the beauty of the naturally distressed walls.

Underscoring this room is an old wooden floor, which also helps to warm up the cool blue walls. Textural elements enhanced by the addition of hanging dried flowers, an oversized coloured glass vase, cushions and a snug armchair complete the look in this informal bohemian dining room.

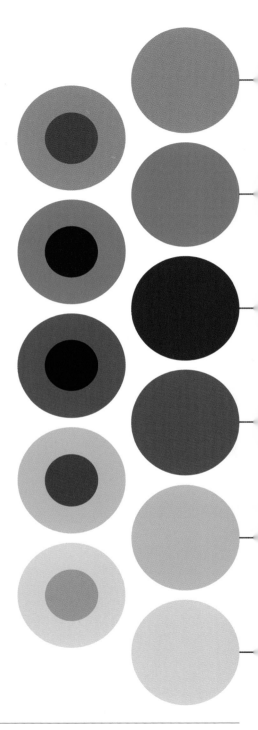

Sideboard

A versatile piece of furniture design, sideboards are often found in a bohemian home. It may seem impossible to think of melding the minimalist clean lines of mid-century pieces with the exuberant, maximalist style of boho, but the juxtaposition of such polar opposites somehow works, and both genres have a lot to offer each other. Vintage is key to bohemian design and the mid-century sideboard can be sourced relatively cheaply and easily. It offers invaluable storage and is a great place to display art, plants and a curated mix of personal collections.

The sideboard opposite is a classic Danish design from the late 1950s and features two drawers and two pull-down cupboards. It is made from teak – a golden wood known for its extreme durability and resistance to woodworm. This sideboard could be used in the dining room, the lounge or even the hallway.

Source
Vinterior
vinterior.co

Material
Teak

Dimensions
Height: 74 cm
Width: 151 cm

Peacock chair

A style icon of the 1960s and 1970s, the peacock chair has been part of our pop culture for decades. Celebrities such as Stevie Nicks and Brigitte Bardot and cult films like *Emmanuelle* have all contributed to its superstardom status.

Made from rattan, the distinctive ornate high-back chair was originally designed as a throne in East Asia. Its sheer size and proportions make it a real statement piece, providing an instant focal point in any room of the house. It is the embodiment of bohemian style.

There are many different styles of peacock chairs, some more embellished than others. The peacock chair opposite features a much-needed linen seat cushion and has a classic shape with a beautiful spiral-like pedestal. The wicker work is delightfully detailed and ornate.

Source
Out There Interiors
outthereinteriors.com

Materials
Rattan

Dimensions
Height: 152 cm
Width: 112 cm

Wall basket

Bring an earthy, ethnic vibe to your bohemian home with one of these intricately handwoven wall baskets from the Hwange district of Zimbabwe, each of which is one-of-a-kind, woven in shades of white and natural palm.

Traditionally these shallow baskets were (and still are) used for winnowing grains, and although they make striking wall art – either displayed alone or when hung together in a group – they can also be used for storing fruit and bread, or for displaying jewellery, soaps or hand towels.

Handwoven from ilala palm and hand-dyed using natural ingredients, this collection is characterized by neutral tones and complex geometric designs, which means each piece can take several days to complete.

Source
The Basket Room
thebasketroom.com

Material
Ilala palm

Dimensions
Diameter: 40 cm
Depth: 9 cm

Tamegroute pottery

Tamegroute is a small village in the south of Morocco close to the Sahara Desert known for legendary green pottery. The workshops, dating as far back as the mid-1600s, remain virtually unchanged with a unique crafting process passed down from generation to generation. Local artisans still work mostly with manual pottery wheels. The clay used for the pottery is sourced from nearby palm groves. The green glaze contains a high proportion of manganese, silica, cobalt, a hint of copper, barley flour and a rock found locally.

Finished pieces are fired in earth kilns giving the pottery its distinctive signature colour, one that never fades even when exposed to heat or humidity. Sometimes, copper is replaced with iron oxide to obtain a more olive brown coloured result. Steeped in tradition and history, Tamegroute pottery includes bowls, mugs, plates and each piece is unique.

Source
Rockett St George
rockettstgeorge.co.uk

Material
Clay

Dimensions
Varies

CLEANSING

The bathroom

Bathrooms have come a long way since their humble beginnings, when they were often no more than just a mere commodity, usually occupying the smallest room in the house. Although the bohemian bathroom is deeply rooted in the past when it comes to the choice of fittings, it is about much more than clinical functionality. It is above all a room of great contrasts: between the simplicity of its fixtures and the mystical, sensual and artistic ambience it reflects. Despite its nonchalant and sometimes even rudimentary appearance, the bohemian bathroom is no afterthought.

Designed for comfort, it is furnished with as much love and attention as any other room in the house. Despite the large quantity of hard surfaces, the bohemian bathroom is first and foremost a tactile space, with the same focus on luxurious accessories, layering of colours, patterns and textures typically seen elsewhere in the home. The juxtaposition of rugs, lace panels, large ornate mirrors, vintage furniture and chandeliers next to the simplest wooden floor and distressed walls creates greater depth to the room, adding an almost whimsical feel to the space.

Sanitary ware

Although it is generally the custom to purchase coordinating bathroom fittings, bohemian-styled bathrooms tend to prefer individually selected pieces. The traditional roll-top bath comes in a vast variety of shapes, sizes and materials, like copper, wood and stone, and is available new or vintage, making this the preferred choice for your tub. It is worth bearing in mind, however, that if you opt for a vintage cast-iron model, you may need to strengthen the floor. Sinks, too, come in a wide variety of designs, and can be wall-hung, inset or

▲ *Comfort is often overlooked in bathrooms. Here the use of rugs and sheepskins softens the hard floor.*

▶ *Heavy brocade curtains are an unusual choice for a bathroom, but they add a feel of luxury to the room.*

▶ *A living wall brings nature indoors and is a perfect way to soak up extra moisture that is often present in a bathroom.*

traditional pedestals. Add an extra bohemian touch by simply sitting your sink on a counter top or on a vintage table-turned-washstand.

Colour

Whilst coloured bathroom suites are few and far between, colour is at the forefront in bohemian design in more ways than just getting a paintbrush out. Tiles are perhaps the most common way to add colour as well as texture in the bathroom. Vintage patterned tiles can convey an air of nostalgia, but they can be on the costly side. Luckily, with today's plethora of high-definition digital printing techniques, several exciting vintage styles can be authentically reproduced at a fraction of the price.

A big part of what makes bohemian design so individual and appealing is the ability to customise and use pieces of furniture for a purpose different to the one originally intended. Consider turning an old chest of drawers or table into a washstand by adapting and re-painting it. You can also customise the roll-top bath by painting the outside in a bold colour. Finally, think about introducing colourful rugs to the bathroom floor. There are many washable options on the market now and they will all provide a splash of colour and texture, as well as giving an unusual touch of luxury to the space.

Lighting

Natural light is always the best kind for a bathroom, as harsh artificial lighting can make daily grooming tasks such as applying make-up, styling hair or shaving much more difficult, but you will nonetheless need some additional task and ambient lighting. The no-rule approach to bohemian design means you can indulge and add drama with a chandelier or a large statement pendant light. There are plenty of bathroom-safe options available on the market these days.

Mirrors

Strategically placed mirrors are by far the best way to maximize natural light and add character to a bathroom. Placed adjacent to the window or on adjoining walls, they brighten the room and provide the illusion of more space. Choose an intricately carved Indian mirror to bring an exotic touch, or maybe a large ornate vintage one, which you can simply lean against a wall. If your bathroom is small, opt for a practical mirrored cupboard to hang above the sink.

Accessories

A bohemian bathroom is more than just a room to wash in – it's a luxurious space for reading and relaxing in the tub. It is also a space to let your personality shine and, as such, it is important to approach decorating it just like any other room of the house. A bohemian bathroom isn't complete without a touch of vintage. Whether it's a mirror or a small trinket box, extend vintage elements to your accessories. Decant bath salts and soaps into pretty glass jars, display vintage perfume bottles, light scented candles. Hang art on the walls, frame prints and photographs, purchase old paintings from thrift stores and use woven baskets as extra

▲ It can be hard to source enough vintage wallpaper to cover a whole room. Here an interlocking design of various pieces of paper has been put together, creating one big patchwork.

storage. Finally, add pieces to connect you with nature such as plants and foliage (see page 38 for suitable plants for bathrooms). Think mismatched pots, repurposed containers and a hanging plant here and there. They will bring the room to life, adding more colour and texture as well as that all-important sense of calm and wellbeing.

Case study

Designer/Owner Jo Wood > **Year(s)** 2017 > **Place** London, UK

In this room, more is definitely more, proving that the bohemian bathroom can be furnished in the same way as any other room of the house. Although the wall colour is fairly neutral, you immediately notice the luxurious feel of this bathroom, and the abundance of varied textures and materials such as wood, tile, glass and linen provides interest and depth to the room.

It is not unusual to see thick-pile rugs, large chandeliers and artwork in bohemian bathrooms, as we do here, and rather than hiding toiletries in bathroom cabinets, everything from apothecary jars to an extensive collection of perfume bottles is on display. The free-standing period bath is the statement piece of the room, lavished by beautiful vintage linens, and a large antique foxed mirror replaces the tiles behind the bath, giving the illusion of space and an added touch of grandeur to the room.

Shower curtain *The shower curtain frames the bath beautifully. Colour has been avoided to draw the eye to the bath.*

Mirror *This mirrored wall gives character to the room and makes it appear larger, reflecting the light all around the room.*

Open shelving *Built-in open shelving is a great way to display the carefully selected bottles and toiletries.*

Chandelier *Although unusual, the choice of lighting emphasizes the feeling of opulence and extravagance ordinarily reserved for the more social rooms of the house.*

Storage *The vintage chest of drawers is both a useful and unexpected choice for a bathroom. It adds valuable storage and another surface to display more personal items.*

Rug *Tiled floors can feel cold underfoot, but this thick piled rug does the trick in warming up the space.*

Signature colours

It can be hard to choose a colour scheme for any small space; white often being favoured for its ability to make a room appear larger and brighter. However, this seemingly windowless bathroom is a perfect example of how it is possible to make a big impact simply through choosing bold colours and plenty of textures.

Here, the pairing of turquoise with the natural hues of terracotta tiles adds warmth, earthiness and personality as well as a distinct Mediterranean vibe. One of the most original characteristics found in rustic terracotta tiles are the irregularities in the finish, which give the room an organic and unique quality so typical in bohemian homes.

The wall tiles have been chosen in a very vibrant shade of turquoise, a colour deeply rooted in human history as one that brings peace, harmony and lasting happiness. Native Americans believed that this colour had the ability to ward off evil and offer health. In the same way, turquoise has been embraced by cultures across the world as one that relaxes the mind and eases mental tension. The combination of the two colours has an invigorating and energising effect.

The earthiness and rustic feel of the scheme are carried through the rest of the room with the use of an unusual wooden basin and rattan accessories. The orange towels echo the colour of the terracotta, whilst the woven light shade casts a warm glow against the tiles.

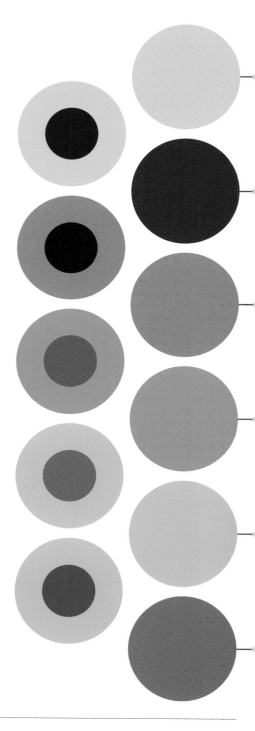

Lace panel

Curtains have been used since ancient times, when animal hides were used for warmth and privacy, but they were nothing like the product we know today. By the Middle Ages, hides had been replaced with cotton and silk, not so much for decorative purposes, but merely to combat the cold. Lace curtains became popular from the mid-19th century at a time when factory-woven lace made such curtains more affordable.

The lace curtains opposite would be the perfect layering piece for windows, doors or even to dress a plain white shower curtain in a bohemian-styled bathroom. They will add texture without blocking the light whilst still giving you some privacy. Dating from the 1940s, similar ones can be found on Etsy or on auction sites for a very reasonable price.

Source
Etsy
etsy.com/uk/shop/FromParisToProvence

Material
Cotton

Dimensions
Length: 125 cm
Width: 59 cm

Display cabinet

Whilst most decorating trends advise you to hide all manner of clutter, the bohemian home likes to display everything and anything on open shelving and in glass cabinets for all to admire. Sturdy and full of character, the rustic wire-sided cupboard opposite has undoubtedly been recycled at some point to achieve this rather quirky look.

There is a certain sense of freedom when it comes to using furniture in boho design, and versatile pieces such as armoires, chests of drawers and display cabinets like this one may not end up serving their original intended purpose. It could be mounted on a wall or simply rest on the floor and would be perfect in a bathroom to display all kinds of perfume bottles, pretty soaps and towels. Of course, it could also be used in the kitchen as a small pantry, as shoe storage in the hallway or even in the children's bedroom as a toy cupboard.

Source
Vinterior
vinterior.co

Material
Wood, wire

Dimensions
Height: 120 cm
Width: 135 cm

Macramé plant holder

Whether you are just dipping your toe into bohemian design or embracing it fully, the macramé plant holder is one of the most iconic boho staples. That 1970s obsession with everything knotted is still as popular today in plant-filled bohemian homes as it was then. A failsafe way to bring texture whilst introducing greenery to your home, there are many variations available to purchase, or, if you are feeling crafty, you could even make one yourself.

Macramé plant hangers work best with trailing houseplants such as fern, ivy or string of pearls. Hang them in groups at different heights to create an interesting and eye-catching display, adding depth, colour and repose to the room.

The plant hanger opposite is plenty long enough to be hung from tall ceilings in the bedroom, the living room or the hallway and is suitable for a wide range of pot sizes due to the expandable nature of macramé.

Source
House Curious
housecurious.co.uk

Material
Cotton

Dimensions
Height: 160 cm
Depth: 20 cm

Copper bath

The copper bath has both character and history, which makes it the perfect addition to your bohemian home. Featured in many of French artist Edgar Degas's paintings, the copper bath was regarded as a luxury item when it first came to prominence. Its opulence and extravagance made it extremely popular with the rich and famous, and figures such as Napoleon and Marie Antoinette are known to have been fans of the design. Imbued with such a rich, colourful and romantic background, the free-standing copper bath makes for a perfect focal point of the bohemian bathroom.

Crafted from hand-poured cast iron, the Tay copper roll-top bath opposite is double-ended and designed to emulate space and luxury. Each bathtub is enamelled by hand up to five times to ensure a clean finish, and, as a final touch, is wrapped in sheets of pure copper, hand-pressed onto the raw cast iron, to ensure durability.

Source
Drummonds
drummonds-uk.com

Material
Copper

Dimensions
Length: 193.5 cm
Height: 55 cm
Width: 86.5 cm

RESTING

The bedroom

The bedroom is the most personal space of any house, but in a bohemian home, the bedroom is also where you can let your imagination run loose and unapologetically show off your personality. Rich in textures, it is always a captivating and creative space without being restricted by practical issues like the other more social rooms in the house. The bohemian bedroom inspires and showcases colours, fabrics and art in a sensuous and sometimes daring way. Like most resting spaces, it is an oasis, but one filled with spirit, individuality and character. Rich colours, global patterns and eclectic decor are some of the hallmarks of a bohemian bedroom. Keepsakes from exotic places turn your space into a relaxing retreat that lets you escape to faraway places. It is a perfect balance between the laid-back, peaceful and eclectic.

The furniture

The bed is usually the focus of the room and is an important investment, as it needs to be above all comfortable. In bohemian bedrooms the bed sits low to the ground and is often a casual affair, providing a striking contrast to the rich and abundant textures that dress it. If you are opting for a bed frame, then wood or rattan are preferred options, both offering charm and rusticity. (If you opt for a pre-owned bed, it is always worth investing in a new mattress to ensure a comfortable night's sleep.) The rest of the bedroom furniture does not need to match in style, period or provenance, so feel free to scour flea markets, antique stores and second-hand shops. An ornate wardrobe from India will look right at home next to an old Victorian armchair.

If you have the space, a seating area on the floor is a fun and extra cosy addition. Simply place some floor cushions on top of a rug or invest in

▲ *For an unusual display hang a beautiful item of clothing as if it were a piece of art.*

▶ *To ramp up the tactile element of a bedroom, layer several rugs, choosing complementing hues or textures for a cohesive look.*

▸ When sticking to a monochrome colour palette, vary the texture for added interest.

▸▸ No need to store all your colourful clothes as they can be proudly displayed in a bohemian bedroom.

a swing chair or hammock to create a wonderful focal point for your bohemian bedroom.

Rugs

Rugs are an essential part of a bohemian bedroom. Depending on your budget, choose an oriental, Persian or Moroccan rug large enough to cover most of the floor (ideally it should sit about halfway under the bed extending out into the room). If you are on a tight budget, consider layering smaller, cheaper rugs to achieve the desired eclectic look. Vary patterns and textures by mixing and matching kilims, ikats, Berbers, cowhides, sisal and thick-pile carpets.

Colours and materials

Boho's penchant for the bright and bold comes into its own in the bedroom, where vivid shades such as red are often featured, providing great impact on the overall scheme without detracting from the bedroom's primary purposes of rest and sleep. The freedom with which bohemians use colour adds to the textural composition of the room, though sometimes the walls are painted in a more subtle, muted shade to create a more calming environment.

The bedroom is the perfect place to indulge in richly patterned textiles, throws and layers of pillows, creating a cosy and comfortable place to retreat to. If you prefer plain bedding, invest in linen that provides textural interest to the scheme. Hang curtains, but not just on windows to diffuse the light; use them to create a canopy around your bed or even to replace cupboard doors.

Accessories

The great part about bohemian style is that you can decorate with basically anything. Beads, feathers, dried plants – absolutely anything goes.

Walls are there to display art and, in the bedroom, this can be an opportunity to showcase paintings and prints that you will have time to fully appreciate in this very personal and reflective space.

Don't keep your most personal items locked away in cupboards. Show them off by displaying your favourite clothes in simple open wardrobes, store shoes in glass cabinets and hang jewellery on a simple piece of driftwood. In a truly bohemian room, every item in the space should have a story behind it.

As we know, plants are a boho staple. Not only do they purify the air, but they also liven up the space and add another layer of colour and texture. Include greenery by hanging trailing plants such as ivy or even the very humble spider plant. Introduce cacti, rubber plants or palms to create your very own mini green oasis in the bedroom.

Lighting

The bedroom lighting needs careful consideration. Use a combination of different styles of lighting to achieve the perfect atmosphere for both day and night. Be sure to include a show-stopping pendant light to provide a consistent amount of light, perhaps adding a dimmer switch to add a cosier feel to the space when needed.

Consider task lighting. Next to the bed, a table or wall lamp is the perfect accompaniment for a late-night read. Pay careful attention to the light bulb, though, as you don't want one that produces a harsh effect.

Finally, fill your bohemian bedroom with soft glowing lanterns, candles and string lights. Hang a cluster of paper lanterns above your bed. On a dresser, display a group of candles in varying heights and colours.

Case study

Designer/Owner Julia Chaplin > **Year(s)** 2015 > **Place** New York, USA

At first glance, this may not look like your typical bohemian bedroom. In fact, it showcases the emergence of a modern take on boho design that features a slightly tamer colour palette and a less maximalist style, where neutral walls are brought to life with the use of texture-heavy furnishings and accessories and bold accents elevate the room.

This bedroom is inspired by the rich tones and intense shades of Moroccan design, from a deep blue carpet that extends all the way to the platform of the bed to the pinks, oranges and browns of the throw and pillows. The addition of a large macramé wall hanging above the bed anchors the space while adding another layer of texture. The hammered metal light is also Moroccan-inspired and provides an interesting variety of tessellating shapes, bringing depth to the scheme as well as a touch of the exotic – a mainstay of bohemian design.

This case study perfectly demonstrates how bohemian style can be as varied as the people behind it. It can be tweaked to suit individual tastes and preferences but still retain the core principles of boho: a unique and personal aesthetic, diversity in colour and texture, a laid-back ambience and a few exotic touches.

Pendant *There are many Moroccan pendants to choose from, all of which will diffuse the light beautifully, casting pretty shadows all over the room.*

Wall hanging *Choose a large macramé hanging to be used as a headboard to create a tactile focal point for the bedroom.*

Personal touches *Mastering the art of bohemian design is all about bringing personal touches like this straw hat.*

Berber rug *Moroccan Berber rugs are a staple of bohemian design. They not only give the room character, but an extra layer of texture.*

Repurposing *The rug used as a bedspread is a perfect example of decorating without rules and boundaries.*

Colour *Wall-to-wall carpets are not often seen in bohemian interiors, but the bright blue shades add intensity to the colour scheme.*

Signature colours

Unlike our case study, this bedroom takes a more traditional approach to the bohemian colour scheme. The vibrancy of the scheme may seem to go against the relaxing, laid-back feel one usually tries to achieve in a bedroom, but the combination of turquoise with the earthier tones of brown and orange shows the owner's love for a very traditional Asian-inspired decor. This cheerful and vivid colour scheme is not for the faint-hearted, and it certainly gives the room a bold, daring and impetuous feel.

Centred around those three main colours, this bohemian bedroom is also rich in textures and clashing patterns, with the addition of a traditional Indian bedspread, a bold Aztec rug and long draping curtains. Deeply rooted in India's culture and history, bohemian interior design not only features rich textiles but also furniture – particularly solid-wood furniture. For an authentic look, make the most of stunning Indian craftsmanship and choose traditional pieces such as the bed shown here. There's a vast variety of distinctive Indian pieces you can pick from, such as wooden chests, wardrobes, mirrors and chairs to give your room an exotic vibe.

The wood panelling and floor have been stained in a similar shade of brown to complement the bed, and the addition of natural materials such as wicker injects extra texture to the room without being overpowering. A bohemian room is never complete without some plant life, and although there are none here, with the doors open the room has a direct connection with the outdoors, so the greenery appears to be an integral part of the interior.

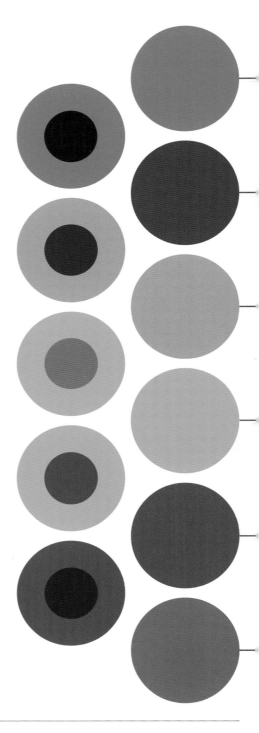

Rattan bed

Rattan, a type of climbing palm tree whose stems are used to make items of furniture, is often seen in bohemian homes in the form of baskets, lampshades and all sorts of indoor and outdoor furniture. Since its beginnings in ancient Egypt, it is a material that has been used extensively throughout the ages, praised for its durable and lightweight qualities. The Victorians delighted in the ornate and decorative possibilities of the material. Fast-forward to the 21st century, and rattan is once more getting the praise it deserves, adorning the rooms of old and new bohemians alike. Due to its popularity, there are now many rattan pieces available both new and second-hand.

The Kinsella rattan bed opposite is the ultimate statement piece for the bohemian bedroom, bringing an element of the exotic with its intricately woven filigree and expansively fanned headboard.

Source
Anthropologie
anthropologie.com

Material
Rattan

Dimensions
Height: 157 cm
Width: 208 cm
Length: 218 cm

Suzani

Steeped in history, the Suzani (seen here as a wall hanging), is an embroidered textile that is a both an essential and versatile component of bohemian design. Suzani originates from the Persian word for needle and was traditionally made for central Asian brides as part of their dowry. They can be traced back to the early 15th century and are rich in colour and intricate in design. Indeed, centuries of needle-crafting tradition has produced endless designs, all lovingly hand-embroidered and featuring a multitude of patterns carrying spiritual and protective messages.

A Suzani can take years to complete and vintage hand-embroidered pieces are rare and costly. There are many machine-made versions these days but, whilst affordable, they have lost the very essence of such a beautiful, ancient craft.

This 'Burning Love Suzani' by La Boheme has been hand-crafted by local artisans and features a distinctive, brightly coloured cotton fabric base with an original hand-embroidered design. Its generous size makes it a multi-functional element of the bohemian home. It can be used as a statement wall hanging, a colourful bed throw or simply draped over a sofa or chair.

Source
La Boheme
thewishingtrees.com

Material
Cotton

Dimensions
Width: 228 cm
Height: 275 cm

Moroccan wedding blanket

Moroccan wedding blankets, also known as
Handiras, have become enormously popular in
the interior design world over the past few years
– so much so that original vintage blankets have
become very hard to find and can cost a small
fortune. Steeped in Berber history, the wedding
blanket, which is essentially a throw, is handed to
a woman upon marriage and forms part of her
dowry. Traditionally, the mother begins hand-
weaving the Handira when her daughter is young.
The weaving itself is a long process and is thought
to bequeath the newlyweds with baraka, or
'blessings'. Once the blanket is woven, it can take
weeks or even months to meticulously attach those
hundreds of mirrored sequins, which are said to
ward off evil.

The Moroccan blanket opposite is a
contemporary take on the traditional Handira.
Woven on wooden looms by expert weavers in
Morocco, it has been dyed in light grey and
embellished with soft cream fringing and silver
sequins. A very traditional bohemian home
accessory, the Handira can be used as a
decorative throw, a cosy blanket, a rug, or
even as a wall hanging.

Source
Bohemia design
bohemiadesign.co.uk

Material
Cotton, wool, sequins

Dimensions
Height: 190 cm
Width: 120 cm

Berber pillow

Originally handwoven by Berber women for their own homes, the Berber kilim cushion comes from the Atlas Mountains in Morocco. With their often complex weaving and bright colours, these cushions bring an ethnic touch to the bohemian home, evoking thoughts of exotic and faraway places. Capturing perfectly the richness of the Berber culture, the tactile design of these cushions adds texture, warmth and sumptuous richness to any room. Cleverly chosen and combined, pillows are the quickest and easiest way to make your room unique and reflect your personality. These pillows are usually one of a kind with varied patterns and colours that you can cleverly combine to achieve an eclectic, worldly look.

The Berber pillow opposite is made of wool and can be layered with different textures and textiles such as silk and cotton and mixed with fringed, tasselled and beaded cushions.

Source
Maison de Marrakech
maisondemarrakech.com

Material
Wool

Dimensions
Length: 38 cm
Width: 32 cm

Kantha quilt

In Sanskrit, the word 'kantha' simply means rags. For centuries, Bengali women have repurposed old saris and cloth scraps to create thin throws which can be used as quilts, blankets and bed covers. Also known as 'nakshi kantha', it is one of the oldest forms of handicrafts practised in India. The quilts are sewn together with a simple running stitch and each is unique in colour and design. The quilts are now popular worldwide and renowned for their eclectic and unique way of recycling and mixing vintage fabrics. Popular in bohemian decor for their rich, cultural heritage and exotic place of origin, they are a useful and versatile accessory.

The colourful kantha quilts opposite have been handmade in India from layers of saris sewn together and feature the traditional kantha stitch. Extra embroidery has sometimes been added and these can be draped on your bed as a throw, used as a curtain or made into a vibrant wall hanging for the bohemian bedroom.

Source
Dassie Artisan
dassieartisan.com

Material
Cotton

Dimensions
Length: 220 cm
Width: 143 cm

Silk lantern

Curiousa & Curiousa design and manufacture hand-blown glass lighting from their studio nestled in Derbyshire's Peak District. Now in their ninth year, they provide bespoke lighting that celebrates colour, quality and form. Their pendants, chandeliers and unique creations can be seen hanging proudly in Harvey Nichols, Liberty London, the Royal Albert Hall, Empire Theatre Liverpool and London Hilton Bankside, and are also available for viewing at their newly opened showroom in Chelsea's Worlds End Studios, London.

Strongly influenced by traditional Chinese lanterns, the Ume lantern, with its luxurious silk tassel, provides a colourful way to celebrate nature inside the bohemian home. Created using designer Esther Patterson's original drawings and paintings of wildflowers and plants, this nature-inspired pendant light would make a bold statement in any bohemian living room or bedroom.

Each light is handmade to order and, as well as the print, you can choose the tassel, flex and fitting to make your Ume lantern a true reflection of your personality and individual taste.

Source
Curiousa & Curiousa
curious.co.uk

Materials
Silk

Dimensions
Width: 86 cm
Height: 42 cm

Further resources

Books:

Abigail Ahern. *Colour: Banish Beige. Boost Colour. Transform Your Home.* Quadrille Publishing Ltd, 2015

Justina Blakeney. *The New Bohemians: Cool and Collected Homes.* Stewart, Tabori & Chang, 2015

Hans Bloomquist. *In the Mood for Colour: Perfect Palettes for Creative Interiors.* Ryland Peters & Small, 2016

Julia Chaplin. *Gypset Living.* Assouline Publishing, 2014

Miguel Flores-Vianna. *Haute Bohemians.* Vendome Press, 2017

Emily Henson. *Bohemian Modern: Imaginative and Affordable Ideas for a Creative and Beautiful Home.* Ryland Peters & Small, 2015

Emily Henson. *Life Unstyled: How to Embrace Imperfection and Create a Home You Love.* Ryland Peters & Small, 2016

Sera Hersham-Loftus. *Seductive Interiors.* CICO Books, 2012

Igor Josifovic and Judith de Graaff. *Urban Jungle: Living and Styling with Plants.* Callwey Verlag, 2016

Annie Sloan. *Annie Sloan Paints Everything.* CICO Books, 2016

Miv Watts. *The Maverick Soul: Inside the Lives & Homes of Eccentric, Eclectic & Free-spirited Bohemians.* Hardie Grant Books, 2017

Websites:

Apartment Therapy
apartmenttherapy.com

Moon to Moon
frommoontomoon.blogspot.com

Jungalow
jungalow.com

SF Girl
sfgirlbybay.com

The Design Files
thedesignfiles.net

La Boheme: House of the Wishing Trees
thewishingtrees.com/blog

Credits

114: Le Creuset, photo courtesy John Lewis
and Partners

118: Maroc Tribal; maroctribal.com

126: Fleamarket Fab/Carly Paige; instagram.com/
fleamarketfab

132: The home of film director Christina Hoglund,
Osterlen, Sweden, © Loupe Images/Debi Treloar

134: modjule ltd.; modjule.co.uk

136: Out There Interiors; outthereinteriors.com

138: The Basket Room; thebasketroom.co.uk

140: Rockett St George; rockettstgeorge.co.uk

145: © Robert Rausch of Gas Design Centre

147: GAP Interiors/Rachael Smith and Victoria
Tunstall

154: windowsofparis.etsy.com

156: vintagefrench.com

160: Drummonds; drummonds-uk.com

164: Fie Frøling; instagram.com/woodlandwhim

173: GAP Interiors/Bureaux, photography by
David Ross

174: Anthropologie; anthropologie.com

178: Bohemia Design; bohemiadesign.com

180: Maison de Marrakech;
maisondemarrakech.com

182: Dassie Artisan; dassieartisan.com

184: Curiousa and Curiousa; curiousa.co.uk

Index

Acknowledgements

I would like to thank HK Living and Los Enamorados Hotel, for kindly supplying a number of the images used in this book.

I also wish to thank all of the people who have contributed to this book. I am very grateful to my followers and the wonderful Instagram community for providing me with constant inspiration and support.

Thank you to Emily and Sorrel for their help and patience, and for making this whole process run smoothly.

Finally, I would like to thank my dear friends and family for all their love and constant encouragement – especially Maddie, Tigerlilly, James and Troy.

Author biography

Kate Young is a freelance interior stylist, blogger, social media influencer and content creator born in France. She fell in love with all things bohemian after a stint travelling the world and immersing herself in a free-spirited lifestyle.

Once settled in the UK, she turned her interior design obsession into her career and started her enormously successful Scandi-Boho blog, Kate Young Design. It was nominated for Cosmopolitan Blog of the Year in 2015 and Kate's home has since been featured in various publications, including *Essential Kitchen, Bathroom and Bedroom Magazine* and blogs such as *abigailahern.com*. She lives with her family in Wiltshire.